I SAW HIS FACE

Powerful Moments of Christ's Mercy

FR. MICHAEL T. MITCHELL, LC

D1218341

ministry23

Published by Ministry23, LLC
2401 Harnish Drive, Ste 100
Algonquin, Illinois 60102
ministry23.com

Scripture quotations (unless otherwise noted) are taken from the Revised Standard Version of the Bible, copyright 1952 [2nd edition, 1971] by the Division of Christian Education of the National Council of the Churches of Christ in the United States of America. Used by permission. All rights reserved.

Where noted, Scripture quotations are taken from the Douay-Rheims Bible copyright © 2009 Saint Benedict Press, LLC. Used by permission. All rights reserved.

Cover Art: Juliana Michelotti

ISBN 978-0-9965812-0-2

Printed in the United States of America

5 4 3 2 1

To my Regnum Christi brothers and sisters

Table of Contents

Introduction

Christ is changing the course of human history and affecting the lives of millions of people. He does so even two thousand years after ascending into heaven and leaving his Church in the hands of the apostles. No single person has affected human history and human lives as he has.

Each and every Christian who takes his or her faith seriously is affected by Christ. It is guaranteed that Christ will make his loving presence felt in one way or another and in varying degrees to each one of us. As I sit in the confessional day after day and from that vantage point glimpse the depths of the human condition, I am truly overjoyed and overwhelmed by how Christ deals so personally and deeply with so many souls. The saga of humanity is only understood in the light of Christ.

I experienced the beauty of Christ in a deep way at a clinic in Port-au-Prince, Haiti. After my ordination to the priesthood in the Regnum Christi Movement as a Legionary of Christ, I was assigned to work in a missionary apostolate called Mission Youth. As chaplain to many university students who give their time as missionaries in third-world countries, I spend about six weeks a year working in the city relief efforts. During these missionary trips to Haiti and just as many trips to Mexico, I have been blessed by many beautiful experiences of Christ which I will share in this book.

One day I found myself at the St. Joseph wounds clinic. Located in central Port-au-Prince, it is a small compound that includes three classrooms and a small medicine dispensary. To get there one must pass through a busy Haitian market. As our vanload of missionaries and two sisters from the Missionaries of Charity squeezed past vendors and shoppers at an agonizingly slow speed, horns were honking, people were shouting, and vendors were hawking everything from water and toothpaste to rat poison. We could have passed more quickly through the market on foot, but our vanload of medical supplies would not have been safe left abandoned in the middle of the market. So we inched along with the vendors parting before us and closing in behind us. After thirty minutes creeping along in this way, we finally arrived at the clinic.

Inside the compound we were met by a difficult sight. In a passageway about eight feet wide and a hundred feet long was a line of sick Haitians waiting to have their bandages removed and their wounds cleaned and rewrapped. These were dirty bandages soaked through with pus, and the emaciated people with many skin diseases not commonly seen by us Americans looked at us imploringly for help.

We were standing amid true suffering, the gray walls and iron gates around us adding to the dismal reality. There was pure misery in this compound, but we could hear liturgical hymns sung in Creole on the other side of the wall, where there was a makeshift open-air chapel that served as a Eucharistic Adoration center. There, over five hundred Haitians were singing and worshiping our Lord in the Eucharist for many hours at a time. Prayer services in Haiti have a charismatic feel to them, as the Haitians love to dance and sing and embellish each song with hand motions and a bit of swaying and turning.

That peaceful music drifted over the walls and provided a beautiful ambiance to the whole compound. However, the sight of the sick and dying was still in marked contrast to the uplifting hymns.

Two of Mother Teresa's nuns were busy getting all the medical supplies ready and so, to distract ourselves from the sight, we busied ourselves with the preparations. There were ten of us and a hundred of them. After a few brief instructions about to how to dress the wounds properly, each of us was given medical gloves and a kit containing the antibiotic creams, gauzes, and dressings we would need. I led the missionaries in a quick prayer and turned to the line of patients.

I must admit I almost got sick when I saw my first patient. He was a middle-aged man, about forty-five years old. His face was wrinkled and worn from hard work in the sun. His body was wasted away from malnourishment, and his skin was covered with blotches and sores. But that was nothing compared to what I noticed next. As I looked down at his wound, I saw elephantiasis for the first time. Due to a parasitic infection, his right leg was almost twice the size of his left. The leg was dressed in a dirty white bandage from the shin down revealing the tips of dirty toes that seemed too large to belong to a human. As my stomach did flip-flops, I forced myself to smile at the man and knelt before him.

Beside me the other missionaries were struggling in similar ways, and as the priest of the group, I forced myself to offer encouragement and support. It quickly proved too much for most of the group, but thankfully they were able to exit the scene gracefully in order to help the sisters inside with a large group of babies that needed medical attention. Four of us were left; two Regnum Christi consecrated women, another missionary who was a nurse, and me. And so we proceeded.

On the sick man's leg, there was no skin from the shin down—only rotted flesh. As a priest, I am a doctor of souls rather than the body. I wasn't sure how to help him, but I tried my best.

I slowly unwound the bandages, which were stuck to his wounds and caused him pain as they were peeled back. Once the bandages were off, I proceeded to clean out the wound with cotton swabs and the solutions provided by the sisters.

After fifteen minutes spent cleaning the wound, I looked up at the man and gave him a smile—*and that was when I saw him.* The eyes of the man looking straight at me smiled back at me. I remembered the line from Scripture in which Christ says: "Truly I tell you, just as you did it to one of the least of these who are members of my family, you did it to me" (Matthew 25:40).

I had an overwhelming sensation at that moment that the man I was attending to was Christ himself. Christ was truly there, and he wanted me to know it. I did not see Christ physically, but spiritually I knew without a doubt that the man I was serving was the Lord Jesus, the second Person of the Holy Trinity.

As the minutes went by, I drifted into another world. The Haitian adoration hymns started echoing deeper in my soul, and I started cleaning out the wound with more love. I was like the woman in the Gospel at the feet of Christ washing him with her tears.

As difficult as dressing that wound was, I did not want it to end. I slowly applied the ointments and took my time binding the leg in gauze and bandages. As I finished up and took off the gloves, I stretched out my hand toward the man and traced the sign of the cross on his forehead. I looked into his eyes and knowing I was seeing Christ, I simply said, "*Merci.* Thank you."

The man stood up and hobbled away. As I finally came out of that mystical state, I saw around me the other missionaries finishing up in silence the wounds of each one of the sick in a similar fashion. There were plenty of tears to go around.

I wanted to find Christ again, so I gathered the kit and sought out the next person in line. I was hungry for more. This time I knelt before a little boy whose foot was run over by a motorcycle, followed by a woman with burns on both her shins, a boy with burns all down his back from falling into a fire, and lastly an old man with only a stump for a foot.

The wounds I saw that day were so repulsive that cleaning them was the hardest thing I have ever done in my life. However, I must say with total sincerity that it was also the most beautiful thing I have ever done. After two hours we were finished; the time had simply flown by. All the while the adoration next door continued. We were all quite somber as we gathered together to leave. Each one knew that at that moment something beautiful had happened. There, in one of the darkest and most miserable places on the planet, Christ had come to dwell. He walked among us for two hours; we felt his presence everywhere, and for a short while we were no longer in Port-au-Prince, Haiti—we were in heaven.

I have since returned many times to that clinic to help dress wounds, and I cherish each and every second I can spend there with Christ. The missionaries I take are always moved to tears. I have seen them embrace the sick and later only stammer as they try to put into words what the experience was like.

Christ is not simply a historical figure from the past. Experiences of Christ such as these are what continue to allow him to shape and change lives two thousand years after his ascension. These experiences, together with the sacraments of the Church, make me love being a Catholic. It pains me to think that so many people don't know who Christ is, who for whatever reason have never experienced him. *A life without Christ makes no sense. A life without Christ ultimately is not worth living. Period.* No wonder we see so much pain and despair around us as liberal humanity continues to run from the Gospel at breakneck speeds and strives to stamp out any mention of God from society.

Vatican II, the twenty-first ecumenical council of the Catholic Church, rightly sums this up: in the *Pastoral Constitution on the Church in the Modern World*:

> *The truth is that only in the mystery of the incarnate Word does the mystery of man take on light. For Adam, the first man, was a figure of Him Who was to come, namely Christ the Lord. Christ, the final Adam, by*

the revelation of the mystery of the Father and His love, **fully reveals man to man himself and makes his supreme calling clear.**[1]

At the end of this book, Christ, the merciful and majestic King, will still be a mystery. No book can encompass him or reveal the depths of his love and mercy for mankind. However, it is my sincere wish that my missionary stories and the Regnum Christi charism I have received will inspire all those who read about them to know the person of Jesus Christ better and to love him more deeply. Our Lord himself sincerely wishes to become part of your life so that through you he may reach many other souls who are lost without him.

Jesus Christ is a treasure that we are called to share with others; he is not a special secret in our lives that we value quietly and keep safely locked up somewhere. Christ longs to be shared with others. May this book be a step in that direction.

---

1 Pope Paul VI, *Gaudium et Spes*, 22 (emphasis added); http://www.vatican.va/archive/hist_ councils/ii_vatican_council/documents/vat-ii_cons_19651207_gaudium-et-spes_en.html.

PART ONE
WHO IS CHRIST?

CHAPTER ONE

Christ and Sinners

O ne of my favorite saints is St. Faustina Kowalska. She had a beautiful relationship with Christ that she carefully detailed in her notebooks. These notebooks were bound together in the now famous book *Diary of Saint Maria Faustina Kowalska: Divine Mercy in My Soul.* When I page through her diary, I can't help but notice how much the Lord loves to forgive sinners and cover them with his mercy. Page after page, the Lord invites Faustina to speak of his mercy, to write of his mercy, and above all to trust in his mercy. In a particularly inspiring text, Jesus tells Faustina that priests need but mention the word "mercy" from the pulpit and the hardest hearts will be moved:

> *The Lord said to me, My daughter, do not tire of proclaiming My mercy. In this way you will refresh this Heart of Mine, which burns with a flame of pity for sinners. Tell My priests that hardened sinners will repent on hearing their words when they speak about My unfathomable mercy, about the compassion I have for them in My Heart. To priests who proclaim and extol My mercy, I will give wondrous power; I will anoint their words and touch the hearts of those to whom they will speak.[1]*

---

1 *Diary of Saint Maria Faustina Kowalska: Divine Mercy in My Soul* (Stockbridge, Mass.: Marian Press, 2010), 1521.

Mercy best describes the beautiful heart of Christ. As a priest I have had many poignant experiences in the confessional that helped me to understand the beauty of Divine Mercy and the depths of God's love. After hours in the confessional spent witnessing the conversion of hearts and tears of repentance, I now understand why Christ so loves being merciful and forgiving.

The Gospels are another place we witness the tender mercy of Christ. He was always available for the crowds, never turning them away even when he was physically exhausted. He wept over Jerusalem and for his lost children. He wished to gather the whole of humanity into his arms. Christ's openness to all peoples and his words of compassion made him a magnet for humanity. Where Christ traveled there were always crowds of people seeking him out.

In the Gospel of John, we find the story of the adulterous woman. Rather than being a story about sin and its consequences or sin and conversion, it is above all a story of the mercy of God. We read:

Jesus went to the Mount of Olives. Early in the morning he came again to the temple. All the people came to him and he sat down and began to teach them. The scribes and the Pharisees brought a woman who had been caught in adultery and made her stand before all of them. (John 8:1–3)

Before Christ made any major decision or did any special work, he usually spent the night in prayer. He knew that he would encounter this poor woman the next morning, and I'm sure he prayed for her to his Father. That morning he would reveal in a special way his love and mercy; he would touch her soul and invite her to a life lived in grace and without sin.

The Pharisees had a hidden agenda. They were using the woman to accomplish two things: Not only did they wish to stone the woman for her sin—through her they also wished to trap the rabbi from Nazareth. If he upheld the law and condemned her, he would contradict his own teaching of love and compassion as well as lose the merciful and kind rabbi image he personified. If he disobeyed the law, then he was just as guilty as the woman, and they would have cause to accuse him.

They said to him, "Teacher, this woman was caught in the very act of committing adultery. Now in the law Moses commanded us to stone such women. Now what do you say?" They said this to test him, so that they might have some charge to bring against him. (John 8:4–6)

The plight of the woman was made even worse by the fact that she alone, and not the man, was suffering the punishment of their sin. She was singled out and the man let free. Who knows the depths of her misery? Who knows what really was happening in her life? She was married, but where is her husband? Where are the witnesses? Was she forced by a passing man into the sin? I don't wish to mitigate her guilt, but surely a quick judgment on her situation would be superficial. The human experience is too deep and complicated to simply condemn on a hasty judgment. This is something I have learned so often in the confessional.

So the woman found herself at the feet of Christ, at the feet of Mercy himself. Little did these scribes and Pharisees know that Christ was about to stun them all. He would surprise them by showing them their *own* sin and broken human nature.

Jesus was quick to respond. His heart immediately went out to the woman, but in his gentleness and majesty, he preferred to deal with her privately, on a personal level. Publicly before the crowd was no way to approach a woman in this situation.

So Jesus bent down into the dust. He lowered himself before all who are present. He began to write on the ground, in words large enough for everyone to see. The image of the Master—God himself—kneeling in the dust and drawing in the sand, must have been a sight to see.

I wish we knew what he wrote, but John is quiet about the details. Down through the centuries various theologians, pastors, and saints have wondered about this same question. It should be noted that Christ wrote with his *finger* on the ground. In the Old Testament, Moses receives the Ten Commandments from God, which God traced with his *finger* onto the stone tablets. When we realize that the same hand that wrote on the tablets also wrote the words on the ground, we can draw our own conclusions. Perhaps Christ began to write out the Ten Commandments before the crowd of people. There in the dust Jesus might have spelled out the laws of the Lord.

When he finished writing the Pharisees were not sure how to interpret Jesus' action, so they ignored the writing and addressed Jesus again. They repeated their question. We read:

> *When they kept on questioning him, he straightened up and said to them,*
> *"Let anyone among you who is without sin be the first to throw a stone*
> *at her." And once again he bent down and wrote on the ground. When*
> *they heard it, they went away, one by one, beginning with the elders; and*
> *Jesus was left alone with the woman standing before him. (John 8:7–9)*

The men went away one by one as Christ bent down to write again. Whatever he wrote on the ground caused each man to reconsider his actions and depart from the scene. I imagine that Christ could have written either a particular sin or a name next to the list of the Ten Commandments. Perhaps the men each saw his own name written out, or a particular sin that he had committed.

Either way the men saw themselves and their own lives written out before them in the dirt. The frailty of their humanity was brought to their awareness. Here they had stood as if innocent and righteous. Yet Christ somehow made them realize that the only difference between them and the woman was that she had been caught. The truth was too much for them to face, and so they turned away. They abandoned Christ, who could have healed them of their plight. Instead they chose to take the wide road that led away from Christ.

A Broken Man Made Whole

Before I return to the woman at Christ's feet, I would like to relay a story that occurred to me within a month of my ordination. I happened to be flying home to Chicago on a two-hour flight. As I boarded the plane and took my seat next to a middle-aged gentleman, I knew something was up; I could sense the need in his soul for Christ. A multitude of sins and deep sorrow in a human heart cannot be hidden. We are made to be with God, living in communion with him. To live far from him in a state of sin is unnatural and does violence to our very being. I sensed immediately that the man desperately needed to talk.

As a fisher of men, I started devising a way to strike up a friendly conversation with the man, but I was hampered by man's new best friend: the iPod. He was "plugged in," and his body language made it clear he did not want to talk. His face, however, depicted a man at war with himself. He wanted to talk, but he was not ready. I had no other choice but to sit and wait and pray. I opened my breviary and started praying.

For the entire two-hour flight, the man paid attention only to his iPod. Toward the end of the flight, as we began our descent, he finally took off the earplugs and headed for the restroom. As he came back I saw my chance and casually ventured a question.

"Headed to Chicago for work?" I asked.

He looked at me and said, "No, I am just passing through on my way out west." And he continued almost immediately: "Father, I'm not right with God—I need to talk with you."

It wasn't news to me that he needed to talk, but his frankness and willingness to do so was surprising. I encouraged him to just let it all out. During the last ten minutes of the flight, he poured out his heart along with a multitude of sins. Suffice to say he was a very broken man, a miserable man. He sought joy and pleasure but never found them—he only dug himself deeper into sin.

As he finished his story, I spoke to him of God's mercy, having the words of Christ to Faustina present in my mind. Tears filled the man's eyes. As the plane touched down, I told the man, "Look, here is what we'll do. Once we get to the gate, we'll go into the terminal and find an empty spot. I will hear your confession, and then once again you will be right with God."

He readily agreed and followed me into the terminal. I found a quiet spot out of earshot of anyone, and we sat down. He made a thorough confession of his sins, and I gave him more words of mercy and encouragement. As I absolved him he was in tears again.

As I made the Sign of the Cross over him, it struck me how beautiful that moment was. Here was a broken man made whole. Here was a human heart full of pain, now soothed and healed. Here was a multitude of vile sins festering in this man's soul, and now he was made clean. Here was a fallen son of God, a child now living in darkness brought into the light. Here was a man once full of pride with many walls and obstacles around his heart that kept Christ out, and now the walls had been torn down and Christ had entered.

Moments like this are some of the most encouraging ones for a priest. I can see why Christ loves being merciful. Only when we are down and out, lost in our sin and weakness, can we truly appreciate the gift of mercy and the beauty of being picked up by a merciful God and pressed close to his heart.

Let's return to the woman at Christ's feet. I see in Christ the same joy that I experience upon bringing a sinner home. He didn't see a broken woman, a sinful person—he saw his own beloved child. She had no idea the amount of love Christ had for her!

When they heard it, they went away, one by one, beginning with the elders; and Jesus was left alone with the woman standing before him. Jesus straightened up and said to her, "Woman, where are they? Has no one condemned you?" (John 8:9–10)

As the woman looked around, she saw only Christ. This is how our judgment will be. When our soul passes from our mortal bodies into eternity, we will be brought into heaven. We will stand before the Lord. There we will be alone with Christ. The world will not be able to accuse us. No one else will have a say—only Christ. Only Christ sees us as we truly are. There, in his eyes, is truth. And the most wonderful reality is that the One who sees us as we are is Mercy himself. Christ told Faustina that before he comes as a just judge, he comes as a King of mercy.

The poor woman in this story only began to grasp the beautiful gift of Divine Mercy.

She said, "No one, sir." And Jesus said, "Neither do I condemn you. Go your way, and from now on do not sin again." (John 8:11)

I pray that these words will be the words of Christ to each one of us. He does not condemn us. We condemn ourselves. To persist in sin is to persist in walking away from God, leaving the house of the Father. God did not create hell; man did. Man creates it every time he walks away from God. When we walk toward Christ, we walk into the arms of heaven.

It is very important to have a Christ-centered approach when we reflect on all that happens to us after our time on Earth is finished. Death is our soul encountering Christ. Our judgment is Christ judging us. Purgatory is Christ purifying us. Heaven is Christ embracing us. Only hell falls outside of Christ. Hell is complete separation from Christ.

The woman before Christ was lifted up. She realized she was a beloved daughter of God. She was made whole; her life was complete. Whatever dark roads she traveled on were now clear and bright because she walked with Christ.

Christ always reaches out his hands to us; he always offers to make the journey of life with us.

With My mercy, I pursue sinners along all their paths, and My Heart rejoices when they return to Me. I forget the bitterness with which they fed My Heart and rejoice at their return.

Tell sinners that no one shall escape My Hand; if they run away from My Merciful Heart, they will fall into My Just hands. Tell sinners that I am always waiting for them, that I listen intently to the beating of their heart... when will it beat for Me?[2]

---

2 *Diary*, 1728.

CHAPTER TWO

Christ and Saints

As great as the saving work of Christ is for us, it would be a terrible mistake to reduce it to simply saving us from sin. There is much more to the Christian story than just salvation. Christ came to call sinners so that, once returned to the sheepfold, sinners could become great saints. He did not come to point an accusing finger and then watch us crawl back to him begging for mercy. His mission was to set ablaze a fire of love on earth that would transform us all into his likeness. Our transformation into Christ is the goal of human existence.

Saving Grace

Some Christian churches completely center around the concept of "saving grace." Such preaching, writings, and hymns reflect a deep desire for salvation and a deep thanksgiving for the removal of their sins by the cross of Christ.

Near my residence in Chicago, there are four Protestant churches. Theses churches have signs out front with motivational messages on them designed to catch the attention of passing motorists. While I understand that the message boards do inspire the occasional soul, I can't help but feel that they do a disservice to Christianity. Most often, these signs convey cute messages about the need to be saved by Jesus. For example:

Walmart is not the only saving place.

All who come in as sinners go out as winners.

Morally bankrupt? God offers instant credit.

Extreme savings offered here—no coupons required.

While the signs may be catchy, the beauty of our faith can't be reduced to a blinking neon sign. Did Christ come to simply make us "winners"? Is the Church a place of "extreme savings" on par with popular department stores? I know the churches that sponsor these signs don't mean to portray a cheap pop culture version of Christianity, but often that is the message received by non-churchgoing passersby.

Much of pop Christian music is also based solely on bringing your sin and weakness to Jesus. With the exception of some great songwriters, the overall message is depressing and goes something like this:

I'm a wretch, I'm too weak, and I'm a disaster. I'm full of sin. But now Jesus has come, and I am saved from my sin and weakness and the wrath of God. I am saved.

The picture this paints is that of millions of souls adrift on a dark and stormy ocean. Jesus passes by in a small boat, scooping the poor sinners out of the water and saving them from drowning. There, in the small boat, soaked to the bone and miserably shaking from the cold, the saved wretches cling to the feet of Christ. The storm goes on, they huddle around Jesus, and then the curtain drops—end of story. Everyone goes to heaven and frolics among the lions and the lambs.

This picture does not do justice to the amazing journey of the spiritual life or the depths of Christ's love for each individual soul. Conversion is only the beginning. Christ pulls us out of the water of sin by dying on the cross out of an immense personal love for us. He then holds us close to his Sacred Heart through the sacraments and transforms us into sons and daughters of his Heavenly Father. By grace we are clothed in the fine robes of the Father, fed with the bread of angels, and allowed to enter into heaven as saints wearing a crown of glory.

Through the gift of sanctifying grace, God calls man to live and radiate love, sharing in his divine life here on earth and completely and for all eternity in heaven. Christ did not come to simply restore the Garden of Eden to its original state; God draws a greater good from evil, not just simply an equal good. He elevated the destiny of humanity by allowing us to become adopted sons and daughters through baptism in his Son. Rather than return us to the original Garden of Eden, he now brings us into the Celestial Garden, the garden of his Church, the Mystical Body of Christ. Heaven is not, as some portray it, a sort of glorified petting zoo. Heaven is spending all eternity in the loving embrace of God the Father!

One's spiritual life does not stop on the day of one's baptism or profound conversion. Those moments are only the beginning of a life of grace. As a Catholic priest, I daily experience on the one hand my own misery and human weakness, and on the other the immense power of God's grace working through me. My brother priests and I are privileged to look into the heart of man through the sacrament of reconciliation. How many souls arrive at our confessional broken and weak! Yet they rise up from their knees strengthened by grace, and over time they grow and are transformed by love. They become tireless apostles with loving hearts, and little by little, they become saints.

Rosali's Story

One little orphan girl I met in Haiti was named Rosali. Abandoned at birth, she had been raised by the loving care of the sisters of the Missionaries of

Charity. Now eight years old, Rosali was dying of HIV. At first there was nothing about her that caught my attention, until one day I saw how she interacted with the other orphans, most of whom are much younger than she.

One afternoon lollipops were passed out to the children who eagerly ripped off the plastic and began to devour the candy. Rosali stuck hers into her pocket for the time being. Later, when the children had finished their candy, Rosali pulled out her own lollipop. The lollipops were quite large, and Rosali broke hers into little pieces. She walked around the playground giving a small piece to each of the other orphans, beginning with the smallest. I was touched by her generosity. The next day I witnessed her do the same thing, this time with a small bag of chips. She never took any for herself, but with motherly care watched over the rest of the orphans.

Orphan children are usually self-centered and defensive. Life has been very harsh to them, and they learn early on to fend for themselves. Where did Rosali get such a big heart? I found the answer minutes later. A sister walked into the orphanage and gathered some of the children around a statue of Mary that was in the playground area. The sister led the children in prayer, making the Sign of the Cross. Rosali was at her side, fervently joining in the prayers. Later I saw her at Mass with the sisters, kneeling as they do, looking to them and copying all their movements and responses during the Mass. Rosali had lived her whole life with these remarkable women. She had learned from them the generosity and love that she poured out upon her fellow orphans.

Rosali's life story could never be summed up by simply being saved from abandonment and living life as a poor orphan. Her life had a second and more beautiful moment, a life transformed by grace, being touched by Christ, becoming each day more like him as she became each day more like the sisters. Rosali, due to her illness, will probably never live long enough to join the sisters by wearing the habit and dedicating her life to the poor. But in my book she is a living saint.

Transforming Grace

The previous chapter ended with the conversion of the sinful woman caught in adultery. She was saved by Christ and made a daughter of God, but her conversion was only the first moment in her life of grace. Afterward she began a journey, following the footsteps of Christ, that led her to sainthood. This second moment is the moment of "transforming grace." To remain at the "saving grace" moment is to truncate Christianity.

The long line of Catholic saints testifies to the beauty of transforming grace and reveal to us that Christianity is not about overcoming vices; it is about growing in virtue and being transformed by the purest love of God. Let us look at several of these saints.

St. Peter

St. Peter is the perfect example of a man who *became* a saint by following Christ and allowing the Lord to work in his life. His first encounter with Christ was in a fisherman's boat. After grudgingly casting his nets to the sea, he was overcome by a great miracle, the miraculous catch of fish. As a seasoned fisherman, Peter knew immediately that this event had a touch of the divine upon it. Deeply humbled, he knelt before Jesus and begged for mercy. Jesus lifted Peter up and invited him to become a fisher of men. At that moment Peter was brought into the light and made a man living for God. His conversion realized, his transformation into *Saint* Peter now began.

In the Gospel we see Peter again and again struggling to love Christ with his whole heart. His weakness still caused him to stumble and fall. He tried to persuade Christ to forego his passion and death, he denied the Master, and he ran from the cross. His remorse on Holy Thursday and Good Friday was a second baptism for him. This was not simply a sorrowful moment when Peter hit rock bottom; his tears were transformative. They were a moment of grace. They led him ultimately to run to the empty tomb on Easter Sunday and to stand up fearlessly before the whole city of Jerusalem on Pentecost.

What would Peter have been without "transforming grace"? His initial encounter with Christ brought him to understand God's role in his life. However, had the miracle not been accompanied by the call to follow Christ, without the subsequent three years of slow transformation by living with the Master, the fisherman Peter would be a forgotten, nameless man who lived around 30 AD. Nothing more.

But *Simon* Peter became *Saint* Peter, the leader of the apostles. He became the fearless disciple of Christ who led the early Church and who gave up his life in painful martyrdom. The "saved" Peter pales in comparison to the "transformed" Peter. Towards the end of his life he wrote in a letter:

Instead, as he who called you is holy, be holy yourselves in all your conduct; for it is written, "You shall be holy, for I am holy." (1 Peter 1:15–16)

But you are a chosen race, a royal priesthood, a holy nation, God's own people, in order that you may proclaim the mighty acts of him who called you out of darkness into his marvelous light. Once you were not a people, but now you are God's people; once you had not received mercy, but now you have received mercy. (1 Peter 2:9–10)

St. Paul

St. Paul is another good example. Before he encountered Christ he was a tent maker from Tarsus, the passionate son of a Pharisee. In Tarsus he was surrounded by Gentile cultures, far from Jerusalem. His close encounters with these Gentiles made him a perfect candidate to become the "Apostle to the Gentiles." As a faithful Jew, his dismay at the whole Jesus of Nazareth event was understandable. Rumors and news have a way of becoming twisted and warped as they spread. News of a new rabbi from Nazareth reached Tarsus— one who performed many signs but also broke the Sabbath. He spoke of destroying the temple. He claimed God was his Father. To the ears of a faithful Jew, this was blasphemy, and any attack on the Temple was an attack on the heart of the Jewish religion.

It is only natural that Saul, as he was originally called, felt righteous indignation at these "Followers of the Way." Then came his initial moment of grace on the road to Damascus. Saul encountered Christ in a mysterious way. He fell to the ground, confronted by a burst of light. Our Lord revealed to Saul that, by attacking his followers, Saul was attacking Christ himself.

After this "saving grace" event in his life, his journey to become *Saint Paul* began. Without transforming grace, Paul might have remained a simple tent maker in Tarsus, but with it he became St. Paul, the apostle *par excellence*. His fire of love grew each day, as did his transformation "into Christ." This fire was poured into his journeys and writings. He was not a man of elegant written words; rather his letters are punchy and strong, full of zeal. They contain many maxims that were the basis of his new life in Christ and the basis of his preaching in the early Church. We read:

I have been crucified with Christ and it is no longer I who live, but it is Christ who lives in me. And the life I now live in the flesh I live by faith in the Son of God, who loved me and gave himself for me. (Galatians 2:20)

He became "another Christ." Later in the letter to the Galatians, Paul alludes to having the "marks of Christ on his body" (Galatians 6:17). Some have interpreted this as a possible allusion to his carrying the stigmata (the physical wounds of Jesus). This is debatable, but what is certain is that, as each day went by, Paul's heart looked more and more like the heart of Christ. Those who encountered Paul encountered the living Christ.

If we go beyond the pages of the New Testament to the saints that have graced the Church down through the ages, we continue to encounter this beautiful reality: Christ is at work in his beloved disciples. *Each soul encounters a unique facet of Christ, and each soul is led down a totally unique pathway to holiness. While they have many resemblances, no two saints are alike and Christ does not want us to repeat the holiness of any other saint.* There are obviously similarities between the saints, but each is unique.

St. Faustina

St. Faustina spoke of her relationship to Christ as entering into a whole new world. She wrote:

> *The interior of my soul is like a large and magnificent world in which God and I live. Except for God, no one is allowed there. At the beginning of this life with God, I was dazzled and overcome with awe. His radiance blinded me, and I thought He was not in my heart; and yet those were the moments when God was working in my soul. Love was becoming purer and stronger, and the Lord brought my will into the closest union with His own holy will. No one will understand what I experience in that splendid place of my soul where I abide constantly with my Beloved.*[1]

The life of grace is a "large and magnificent world" for us to explore. The more we go into prayer and go deeper into the spiritual life, the more this

---

1 *Diary*, 582

world opens up before us. So many people never reach this understanding because the noise of our culture and the frantic pace of life keep them from ever sinking into the depths of God's love. They race and skip over the surface of life so quickly that they never have time to ponder and pray.

St. John of the Cross

In my opinion, the saint who most masterfully explains the spiritual life is St. John of the Cross. His poems of love are some of the most beautiful in Christian literature. *Only through a deep love can a follower of Christ enter into his Heart and detect his deepest feelings, his liveliest desires and the intensity of his love.* John of the Cross did this masterfully in his lifetime, and his works radiate the love of Christ. His writings have such a depth to them that one may not find them particularly helpful in the beginning. In his poem "Living Flame of Love," he writes:

> *O living flame of love*
> *that tenderly wounds my soul*
> *in its deepest center! Since*
> *now you are not oppressive,*
> *now consummate! if it be your will:*
> *tear through the veil of this sweet encounter!* [2]

The living flame of love is Divine Love. The image St. John used to explain this poem is a log of wood thrown on the fire. At first the log is burned and blackened. This is the moment of the spiritual life when the soul rids itself of vices; it is the moment of dying to self. Little by little it begins to heat up until it becomes enflamed and burns. This signifies much activity; the flames

---

2 John of the Cross, *Living Flame of Love*.

sweep over the wood and resemble the soul alive in many virtues and good works. Then at last the flames die down and the log glows ardently, at its hottest temperature and peacefully transmitting its light and heat to all around it.

One can just see St. John of the Cross in the cold and windswept region of Castilla in Spain throwing another log onto his hearth and watching this pattern repeat itself over and over again. This is how the soul approaches God: first it burns, then it is enflamed, and finally it glows. He ends his poem with this stanza:

> How gently and lovingly
> you wake in my heart,
> where in secret you dwell alone;
> and in your sweet breathing,
> filled with good and glory,
> how tenderly you swell my heart with love.[3]

A saint has a heart that swells with love. This love impels the soul to great and marvelous works. *The goal of our lives must be Christ—to know him, love him, follow him, and make him known to others.* This love frees the soul. As children of God, nothing hinders our souls or ever takes away our peace. Imprisonment can't stop us from loving. Sickness can't stop us from preaching Christ. In all things, it is Christ who lives and moves in us. Our experience of God's love in Christ necessarily becomes something living. For Christians, experiencing Christ deeply means living *in* love, living *to* love, and nourishing our life *on* love. Our lives can have no other motivation, meaning, or goal than Christian love.

---

3 John of the Cross, *Living Flame of Love.*

CHAPTER THREE

Christ on the Island

Christ is revealed most fully in his post-resurrection glory. Before his passion and death, Christ's glory was hidden in his humanity. Although his public life provides some glimpses of his glory in the many miracles and in his transfiguration, it is only when Christ rose from the dead that his glorified personhood shone forth.

There is something awe-inspiring and beautiful about Christ, even before his resurrection. But on Easter Sunday Jesus Christ, both divine and human, both eternal and majestic, truly shines forth in all his splendor.

When we contemplate Christ, the eternal and kingly dimension of his person can never be forgotten. There is something seriously missing in the "gentle Jesus," the "hippy Jesus," and the "political Jesus" that have been at times presented to us.

To know Jesus you must know him as he truly is: the Alpha and the Omega. This is the Jesus we will meet in the next three chapters. We will begin with an appearance of our Lord to St. John the Evangelist.

THE BELOVED DISCIPLE

The martyrdom of St. John the Evangelist was in one sense the hardest martyrdom of any of the apostles. John was not actually martyred in the strict sense of the word. Instead his life was a slow martyrdom, a gradual outpouring of self.

John was the youngest of the apostles. It is thought he was around sixteen years of age when Jesus first crossed his path, just barely a man. Yet Christ chose him for an immense work and eventually included him among his close friends, giving him the honorable title of Apostle of the Church.

St. John is known as the Beloved Disciple, the one whose purity and childlike simplicity allowed him to participate more deeply in the inner life of Christ, able to read into Christ's heart's feelings and desires. While some of the apostles were a bit rough around the edges, just common fishermen, John had important family connections in Jerusalem; he had most likely studied the law and was spiritually very perceptive. He understood our Lord on a deeper level than most of the other apostles did at first. Thus Jesus graced John with some special gifts: He invited John to accompany him up Mt. Tabor to witness the Transfiguration, lay his head on his chest at the last supper, and join him in prayer in the garden of Gethsemane.

John loved our Lord with all his heart and never wanted to leave him. He alone of the apostles made it to the foot of the cross. His overwhelming desire to be with Christ made his slow martyrdom of witnessing and loving on earth so difficult. According to tradition, he died at a very old age, somewhere around 100, which means he had to spend the last seventy-five years of his life waiting to finally see his friend and Lord again. And this—for someone who so dearly wanted to be with Christ—was a most unbearable martyrdom. He had to wait in patience and faith to finally be reunited with his beloved Lord.

John knew that his struggles as an exile on the island of Patmos were part of the cross he was asked to carry. Having stood at Mary's side on the hill of Calvary on Good Friday, John understood the meaning of the cross like few others. He understood that the cross was a necessary part of human life, and therefore he embraced his own cross, the sufferings God allowed in his life, just as he had seen his Lord do many years earlier.

However, as he daily followed his Master's example on Calvary, he did have a few consolations along the way. One of them happened on the island of Patmos. John had been exiled there and spent many years of his life praying and writing letters, far from his disciples and fellow Christians. He wished to love the Church and serve her as best he could, even while far from her. *A true disciple of Christ is one who loves Christ, loves all that Christ loves, specifically the Father, the Church, and souls.*

The island of John's exile itself was not very large and quite bare. In those stark circumstances, one can imagine that John would have spent most of his days in prayer, united spiritually with his beloved Lord. As a true disciple of the Lord, John was in love with the Church. Proof of this is the fact that he continually wrote letters to keep the flock of Christ motivated. Some of those letters made their way into the New Testament, as did the vision he saw while on the Isle of Patmos: the Book of Revelation. Due to being written at a later date, his Gospel is by far the most theologically rich of the four. His years of reflection and prayer in exile were certainly poured into that work with the guidance of the Holy Spirit.

After years on the tiny island, I am sure St. John would have been happy to have read a book by another St. John. Centuries later we encounter St. John of the Cross, a sixteenth-century Carmelite friar and mystic from Spain, who wrote a book entitled *The Spiritual Canticle*. In it he describes many images to explain the personal encounter with Christ, the Beloved. One image is quite intriguing and would have been readily understood by St. John the Evangelist: St. John of the Cross called Christ an "exotic island." We read in *The Spiritual Canticle*:

My Beloved,
the mountains
and lonely wooded valleys,
exotic islands,
and resounding rivers,

the whistling of love-stirring breezes,

the tranquil night

at the time of the rising dawn,

silent music,

sounding solitude,

the supper that refreshes, and deepens love.[1]

St. John of the Cross explained later that Jesus is an exotic island, where, far from common things, one finds true uniqueness. The plants and animals on distant islands are different from what is found on the mainland. While the mainland is predictable, known, routine, and commonplace, the exotic islands far offshore are mysterious and unknown. Encountering one amid the violent and dangerous ocean is a safe haven. Exploring one is a new adventure and a memorable experience—and so is the encounter with Christ. When we find Jesus Christ, we find uniqueness and newness. He is totally *other*. He breaks the monotony of life lived routinely and without meaning. He enriches life in a unique way for each person.

In fact, every soul is called to encounter Christ in a new and unique way. Just as no two saints have the same experience of Christ, so no two souls will experience Christ in the same way. Christ is always new, always unique, always eternal. As God he is at once knowable yet infinitely *unknowable*. There is always more beauty to explore in Christ; he is inexhaustible. We will spend all of eternity knowing and loving him. *Every person who embarks on the spiritual life will find in Christ an "exotic island" that will be his or hers to explore, a whole universe.* The union of God and the soul creates a universe where both dwell in light and love.

One Sunday morning, as the Apostle John was beginning his morning

---

1 St. John of the Cross, *Spiritual Canticle*, stanzas 14–15.

prayer, he had a special experience of Christ that he wrote down for us; it deserves a lot of meditation.

It was the Lord's Day, and as Christ's flock was gathering to celebrate the Eucharist together, John was probably casting his mind across the sea to them. He says he was "in the Spirit," meaning the Holy Spirit was in his soul strongly praying through him with the greatest longings a human heart could ever have. He wished to join his brethren across the sea, but more than anything he wished to join Christ eternally in heaven.

Suddenly a loud voice boomed from behind him like a trumpet. He wrote:

I was in the spirit on the Lord's day, and I heard behind me a loud voice like a trumpet saying, "Write in a book what you see and send it to the seven churches, to Ephesus, to Smyrna, to Pergamum, to Thyatira, to Sardis, to Philadelphia, and to Laodicea."

Then I turned to see whose voice it was that spoke to me, and on turning I saw seven golden lampstands, and in the midst of the lampstands I saw one like the Son of Man, clothed with a long robe and with a golden sash across his chest. His head and his hair were white as white wool, white as snow; his eyes were like a flame of fire, his feet were like burnished bronze, refined as in a furnace, and his voice was like the sound of many waters. In his right hand he held seven stars, and from his mouth came a sharp, two-edged sword, and his face was like the sun shining with full force. (Revelation 1:10–16)

Gone are the weaknesses and limits of Jesus's human nature. Now he comes in the clouds, filled with light. He stands amid seven gold lampstands, which symbolize the churches. The symbolic number seven signifies fullness and completion and therefore means the full number of churches. His words are

I SAW HIS FACE

not just meant for the churches of his time, but for all churches of all times. Christ's words are everlasting.

Here is Christ as he truly is in all his glory. His voice is thunder; his face shines like the sun. Christ is revealed, not just with godlike *qualities;* he *is* God, and all else is understood only in relation to him.

CHRIST'S RIGHT ARM OF POWER

The right arm is always a symbol of power in the Bible. God's right arm is God's power and omnipotence. It is significant that John describes the arm of Christ in the continuation of the passage.

> *When I saw him, I fell at his feet as though dead. But he placed his right hand on me, saying, "Do not be afraid; I am the first and the last, and the living one. I was dead, and see, I am alive forever and ever; and I have the keys of Death and of Hades. (Revelation 1:17–18)*

Notice how majestic and eternal the words of Christ ring out! He is the Beginning and the End, the First and the Last. Notice how he is wearing a vestment of white, a sash of gold. He is the eternal High Priest interceding for us forever at the right hand of the Father. Notice how his face is shining like the sun, his eyes like fire. This Christ is a far cry from the hip Jesus, the good guy Jesus, or the moralist teacher Jesus that some promote.

As John kneels before Christ, Christ lays his arm on John. He touches him with his arm of power. John, who has come to understand the very depths and the beauty of Christ's heart, knows how unworthy he is to be in the presence of his Beloved. He becomes like the soul in the Song of Songs who, when encountering the Beloved, says: "My soul failed me when he spoke" (Song of Songs 5:6).

However, even in all his glory, Christ does not provoke fear; instead he draws all men to himself. As John falls before him in his humility, Christ lays his right hand upon him, his right arm of power. He assures John that he need not be afraid.

John relayed this experience at the beginning of the Book of Revelation. It is the last book of the Bible and contains the last words of Christ and the last prophecies for the Church. John prepared his readers by including this experience in the first chapter. Just as Christ prepared him to receive the revelations, so John prepared us.

This passage tells us much about Christ. When we pray to him, we must see him in all his glory. Of course, we can feel his closeness when he explained the Father's great love in the parable of the prodigal son. We can feel his closeness when he explained how he carries lost sheep on his shoulders. We can feel his agony while with him in Gethsemane. But through all of this, *we need to allow Christ to touch us with his right arm of power.*

This moment of grace happens when we freely open our soul to Christ with the humble simplicity of a child. Christ is God; we are his children. Each one of us needs to kneel before Christ in his glory. Everything we have is from him. We are going to return to him. John on Patmos had nothing. His stark empty island gave him little consolation; it was a difficult cross to carry. Yet in prayer before his Lord, he had everything. He was wrapped in ecstasy before the Lord of Lords and the King of Kings. John did not bemoan his many crosses or sufferings—he saw them as preparation for the divine encounter.

On our "exotic island" we will also find a cross. Many times when the cross comes our way, we stay focused only on the negative—on the act of carrying the cross. We focus on Calvary alone. There is nothing wrong with focusing on the cross and Calvary, but we aren't meant to stay there.

AN EASTER PEOPLE

It is true that to get to Easter Sunday, we must follow Christ through Good

Friday. *But we are not a Church of Good Friday, we are a Church of Easter Sunday!* The laments and sharp chants of Good Friday move us and at times the cross speaks more to us in our human misery. But ultimately we need to step into the light and join Christ in his glory.

Let us turn again to St. Faustina. Christ once revealed a beautiful truth about the cross and suffering to her. In her diary she recorded a vision she had of Jesus and his words to her about the cross. She wrote:

> *Then I saw the Lord Jesus nailed to the cross. When He had hung on it for a while, I saw a multitude of souls crucified like Him. Then I saw a second multitude of souls, and a third. The second multitude were not nailed to their crosses, but were holding them firmly in their hands. The third were neither nailed to their crosses nor holding them firmly in their hands, but were dragging their crosses behind them and were discontent. Jesus then said to me,* **Do you see these souls? Those who are like Me in the pain and contempt they suffer will be like Me also in glory. And those who resemble Me less in pain and contempt will also bear less resemblance to Me in glory.**[2]

Those who carry their cross like Christ will shine like Christ in his glory. Christ did not despair before his cross; he embraced it and kissed it and walked toward Calvary with his eyes set on his Father. He saw the glory of the Father and the Father's love for him.

The next time you find a cross on *your* island, embrace it and look more toward the eternal meaning of that cross than its present earthly troubles. And the next time you go to prayer, kneel before Christ in his glory, the Alpha and the Omega, and allow his right arm of power to help you carry your cross.

---

2 *Diary*, 446.

CHAPTER FOUR

Christ on the Road

E veryone needs a personal experience of Christ and his merciful and life-giving love. This is a need rooted in the depths of every human heart. Christ answers this need by coming out to meet us, by crossing our path. He wishes to initiate this encounter and seeks moments when our hearts are more open and disposed to welcome him. He is the Beloved from the Song of Songs of whom the bride says:

> *Look, there he stands*
> *behind our wall,*
> *gazing in at the windows,*
> *looking through the lattice.*
> *My beloved speaks and says to me:*
> *"Arise, my love, my fair one,*
> *and come away." (Song of Songs 2:9–10)*

Christ is looking into the window of your heart. Christ loves to walk with you. He journeys alongside you—at times carrying you, and at other times running with you or letting you lean on him. Your journey is his journey and vice versa.

In the Gospels many times we see Christ walking with his disciples.

Sometimes it was on a long journey, such as the time when he had to rest by the well in the Samaritan village. Other times it was a short walk from the upper room to the garden of Gethsemane.

The story of the journey of the two disciples on the road to Emmaus has long been my favorite passage to meditate on. It has so many nuances that no one book can exhaust them. Here again we see our Lord walking with two of the disciples. This time, however, they don't realize it is Christ.

The story began on a stretch of road between Jerusalem and Emmaus, a seven-mile journey, and took place early on the first morning of the Resurrection. However, the full truth of the Resurrection was not yet entirely known.

These two disciples, one named Cleopas, were on their way back home. They had been in Jerusalem for the feasts, and now they wanted to return to their families. They were disciples of our Lord, and they had expected great signs from Jesus that Passover. Yet all their hopes were dashed; Jesus had been defeated.

So we have two very heavyhearted men walking on the road, hoping to find some consolation in returning home to their livelihood. It is at this precise moment, when they are downtrodden and in need of Christ's presence, that Christ comes their way. Our Lord always comes to our side in trials, though he doesn't necessarily take away trials or crosses, and at times he actually leads us to them.

Christ was again in his post-resurrection glory. However, this time he chose to hide his glory. He adopted the image of a "foreigner," one who was simply visiting Jerusalem, a pilgrim like so many others. Theologians speculate as to why Jesus looked so different in this moment—so different that he may not have looked Jewish at all. Christ could very well have taken on a human appearance that was no longer confined to one race. He was now a Man for all men.

The disciples made it clear that what was on their hearts is the life and death of Jesus, the rabbi who they hoped would throw off the yoke of the Romans. They secretly hoped that Jesus of Nazareth would solve all the problems of the Jewish people. Now they were on their way home, half in a daze at what to make of life and at a loss regarding their next steps.

Christ began to reveal himself. He made the most of the seven-mile trip, speaking to them about all the Scriptures concerning himself. This was the first "Bible study," and God himself was the teacher! How many theologians today wish they could have been there to soak up every word, every story, and every interpretation that came from the lips of Christ!

Christ walked with these two disciples for seven miles, which could have taken around three hours. We can assume they started mid-morning, since the disciples already knew of the empty tomb and had doubtless lingered a bit in the city to try and understand what had happened. Just imagine Christ's gentle voice revealing mystery upon mystery to these fortunate men for over three hours!

Christ most likely started with Genesis, focusing on the great typology of the Old Testament. He spoke to them about God the Father desiring to save mankind from sin. He mentioned the enmity between the snake and the woman and explained how Mary his mother was precisely that woman. He referred to the serpent in the desert and how it prefigured his cross. He spoke about the suffering servant in Isaiah, the prophecy of his birth in Bethlehem. In short, Christ would have covered the entire Old Testament and opened their minds to God's infinite wisdom and divine plans.

The words of Christ were gentle yet strong, easy to understand yet with an eternal ring of truth to them. As they listened, the two disciples' hearts began to burn with enthusiasm and renewed joy. They were enthralled with Christ's preaching; the Word of God was alive and active in their hearts. They were now on fire, and thus Christ knew they were ready for another and greater revelation.

As they approached Emmaus, Christ indicated that he was going on a little farther. *Christ never imposes his will. He is always in the soul as an invited guest. He does not want to force any of us to accept him; instead he respects the beautiful gift of freedom we have been given.*

The two disciples picked up on Jesus's plans to continue on his journey and would have nothing of it. They wanted Christ. They desired his presence even when they didn't recognize him. *Every person needs a personal encounter with Christ and his merciful and life-giving love. This is a need rooted in the depths of every human heart.* How many souls are out there today that don't know Christ but whose hearts desire his love and grace! It is up to us—the disciples of today—to bring Christ to this thirsting world!

Christ was easily persuaded to remain with the disciples that evening, as the sun was setting and the day was almost over. In fact, this is what he most desired in his heart: the invitation to make his home with his beloved children. One of God's greatest gifts revealed to us in Christ is how much God wants to dwell with us. We do not merit this grace. Despite our unworthiness of this blessing, Christ makes it clear he desires our friendship. Our Lord wishes to be with us, to fight for us, to die for us. He did so on the cross and continues to do so at every Mass where he comes to dwell in the Blessed Sacrament. However, he always stops short of demanding our love. His actions reveal how much he desires our love, but he never commands it. Love cannot be forced. That is why every Christian who freely welcomes Christ in prayer brings delight to the Sacred Heart of Christ.

A Sanctuary for the Lord

In Haiti I met a little two-year-old boy who welcomed Christ into his heart in a wonderful way. He was in a clinic for sick children run by the Missionaries of Charity. The little boy was very ill and his chances of survival pretty slim. The missionaries and I took turns holding the boy, helping to keep him comfortable and warm. During the morning the missionaries had been singing songs to the babies in the cribs. One of the songs was "Lord, prepare me to be a sanctuary." It is a common praise and worship song that is particularly beautiful in the context of the Eucharist, where each one of us becomes a sanctuary for our Lord.

In the afternoon, as we continued our care of the children, one of the missionaries took the little boy into his arms and sat with him for a few hours. As the little boy's breathing grew slower and his body weakened, it was obvious his time on earth was short. Suddenly, the boy began to hum and sing the song, "Lord, prepare me to be a sanctuary." Imagine the effect this had on the missionary! He was quickly brought to tears as he held this little boy who was praying (albeit unknowingly) to become a holy sanctuary for Christ. The boy did not understand English; Creole would have been his native language. He was simply singing and repeating the song he had heard from the missionaries that morning. He died that evening. Here was a little boy about to meet Christ, who with his whole being prayed to become a worthy sanctuary. Our Lord reminds us in the Gospel of Matthew:

> *And Jesus said to them: Yea, have you never read: Out of the mouth of infants and of sucklings thou hast perfected praise? (Matthew 21:16)*

After their long journey, Christ was ready to join these two disciples for a moment's respite and food. By welcoming Christ, they too have expressed the desire to be a sanctuary for the Lord. Together they entered into the dwelling place—the two disciples and their Guest.

Gathered around the Altar

Christ sat with them at table. After encountering each other in the Liturgy of the Word, they proceeded into the Liturgy of the Eucharist as the Mass unfolds throughout the passage. First there was the greeting along the way of life, the reading of the Word of God, the homily, and then they entered into the sanctuary and sat around the altar. Christ the high Priest took the bread, blessed it, and broke it.

The two disciples suddenly recognized Christ. He allowed them this brief grace, and for an instant Christ was there before them handing them a piece of bread, which is actually his Body and Blood. Mesmerized by the beauty of Christ and taking the bread almost without thinking, Christ disappeared from their sight. Although he didn't totally disappear, his appearance changed. He remained present, Body and Blood, Soul and Divinity, in their hands. They looked down at that bread, and the Gospel says they "recognized him."

In the Eucharist devout Catholics also "recognize" Christ! The beauty of his presence is so amazing, so awesome, that you will find in every parish many souls who spend long hours in prayer before the Blessed Sacrament. Hidden in the host just inside the tabernacle, Christ stands as in the Song of Songs, peering through the monstrance and beckoning us to come to him. The Eucharist is truly a window into another world.

Cleopas and his friend consumed the host and were united in a special way to the Lord. I imagine how they must have looked at one another in shock, awe, and exuberant joy. They had been with Christ, and their hearts had been burning all day!

They did then what we always do after Mass. The priest tells us: "Go and proclaim the good news!"

They left their resting place in Emmaus and went out to proclaim the good news, hurrying back to Jerusalem. They arrived breathless and tired, but so overcome with joy that the journey had seemed to take only a moment.

There, surrounded by the apostles and seeing the Blessed Mother, that "Woman" from Genesis, they told their special story. The apostles shared their stories as well, and the first community began to grow in love and hope. Christ had truly risen!

The story of Emmaus underlines the beautiful way in which Christ comes out to meet his flock. He desires to cross our path, at times openly but more often in secret. Christ is disguised in our family and friends, in the joys and sorrows of life. He shares them all with us.

Many Christians desire to see Christ, to hear his voice and see his face. The secret is found in the Eucharistic feast. Just as for the two disciples of Emmaus, all may find Christ in the breaking of the bread. Only with the Eucharist in their hands did the disciples' eyes penetrate into the mystery of Christ. Christ *wants* to reveal himself to us.

God the Father has revealed his love for us in Christ, the historical and tangible expression of this love. Therefore to experience God's love, we must fix our eyes on the face of Christ. Catholics that often receive Christ in Communion are souls that are able to see Christ everywhere. They become simple and pure souls whose eyes already penetrate eternity while they remain living in time.

CHAPTER FIVE

Christ in the Upper Room

After the resurrection, Christ appeared in the upper room to the disciples, as we read in the Gospels of Luke and John. Both Gospels reveal Christ again in his post-resurrection glory. He was the same yet totally different. He appeared as the Alpha and the Omega, awesome in his eternal being. His victory was definite and everlasting. He desired that the disciples proclaim this to the whole world. Thus he went to the upper room where he knew he would find his flock huddled together in prayer.

The upper room became the center and heart of the early Church. It was the first cathedral. Initially it was simply a refuge and a hideout. The apostles were understandably wary of their immediate future. The death of our Lord could well have been the beginning of a plan by the Jewish authorities to rid Jerusalem of all followers of Christ, starting first with Jesus of Nazareth and continuing with the apostles. Because of this they hid themselves, much like Adam and Eve after the fall.

After Christ's death on the cross, the apostles were scared and alone, like sheep without a shepherd. Whereas before they had peace and security alongside the Lord, now they had fear and confusion. The upper room was the place they last shared a Passover meal with Christ. It was there that he spoke from his heart and revealed just how much he loved them. Like little children, they took shelter from the dark and dangerous streets of Jerusalem and went back to that upper room, wishing that the unfortunate turn of events could somehow be undone.

They were souls adrift, men without purpose. Place yourself for a moment in their position. Their hopes and dreams have been dashed. Gone was the beautiful life in the company of Jesus of Nazareth that had opened up for them for the last three years. The dreams of success and peace alongside the Miracle Worker of Nazareth were now empty, lost in the past. The cold, hard reality pressed in upon them, and their hearts were heavy.

The upper room, which only hours before had been a place of joyful singing, was now dark. They had no idea where God was leading them. Many of the apostles felt sorrow for abandoning the Master in his time of need, for not being there when he needed them the most. They are souls who started out upon the divine road to holiness and life with God only to be overwhelmed by discouragement when they were only halfway there.

Souls Adrift

The upper room before Pentecost is symbolic of a certain type of soul. Not souls on the wide road of sin, but souls who are adrift. These are not prodigal sons in foreign lands, despairing amid the swine. No, these are good and noble souls who faithfully have followed the Master. Yet at a certain point, the path became dark, the road uncertain. After years in his service, trials and routine have set in. Perhaps these souls are more like the older son in the parable of the prodigal son who dedicated his life to the father, but more because of what he received than from a deep love for his father.

After the cross and before the Risen Christ appears, *the upper room is symbolic of a state of spiritual dryness.* Any Christian who has gone through a period of darkness and trial understands this "upper room." They are the priests who, after years of ministry, seem to see little or no fruit and become discouraged. They are the religious sisters and consecrated women who feel their years of service have gone unnoticed and unappreciated, their struggle for perfection seemingly unattainable. They are the married couples who have lost a child or whose financial difficulties appear insurmountable. At some point these souls generously surrendered their lives to Christ and began walking down the narrow road of perfection. At a later point on that road the cross of Christ came their way. At the sight of this cross, their world comes crashing down. The road appears impossible, and Christ seems far away.

Yet the upper room of spiritual darkness is precisely where Christ comes to meet them. Like the disciples on the road to Emmaus, Christ always walks with us, even when we don't feel his presence. In the upper room Christ is present to every suffering Christian, even when at times his presence is hidden. When a soul turns to Christ in the depths of prayer, Christ is able to carry the soul and support it amid these trials.

St. Faustina had her share of trials, and one day she wrote in her diary:

*Once when I was being crushed by dreadful sufferings, I went into the chapel and said from the bottom of my soul, "Do what You will with me, O Jesus; I will adore You in everything. May Your will be done in me, O my Lord and my God, and I will praise Your infinite mercy." Through this act of submission, the terrible torments left me. Suddenly I saw Jesus, who said to me, **I am always in your heart.** An inconceivable joy entered my soul, and a great love of God set my heart aflame. I see that God never tries us beyond what we are able to suffer. Oh, I fear nothing; if God sends such great suffering to a soul, He upholds it with an even greater grace, although we are not aware of it. One act of trust at such moments gives greater glory to God than whole hours passed in prayer filled with consolations.[1]*

---

1 *Diary*, 78.

We can learn much from the attitude of the disciples. In these trying times, the upper room became a place of prayer. Here the disciples gathered to break bread and offer hymns and psalms to God. They drew strength from this liturgy—strength enough to face the fears and dangers that surrounded them.

It also became a place of Marian devotion. The Book of Acts tells us that they persevered in prayer together with Mary. The Blessed Mother without a doubt began in earnest to take on her new responsibility as Mother of the Church. Christ had told her from the cross that she, the Woman, was now the Mother. John, the beloved disciple, surely transmitted this joyful message to all the apostles and disciples. He was the first and most devoted son of Mary, much as Christ was. One can imagine Mary sitting down among the disciples in the upper room and telling them all about Jesus—his hidden life, his compassion for humanity. She became a focal point for the Church.

God never wishes to leave us in our fears; he always takes that first step of grace toward us. Just as when God the Father walked through the garden in the evening in search of a fearful Adam and Eve, so Christ now enters the upper room in search of his fearful disciples. God forever loves to come and walk alongside mankind. It is one of his greatest delights.

Our Lord's first reaction could have been to scold the apostles for their lack of faith. The last time he saw them was before he died when they abandoned him before a small army of men. They left him alone to accept his fate. Three years of life together had not been enough for the apostles to choose to embrace the same fate as the Master. Christ would have been justified to show a righteous anger toward them, and undoubtedly in his human heart felt sorrow at having been abandoned by his closest friends.

Thomas à Kempis rightly observes in his book *The Imitation of Christ* that everyone loves to be with Christ in the joyful moments of the miracles and on Mt. Tabor. Few, however, follow the Master on the royal road to Calvary. Accepting the cross has no appeal to our human nature, which is wounded by sin. Yet it remains a necessary avenue to holiness and apostolic effectiveness. *The cross was the path Christ himself chose to fulfill his work, and it is the path he chooses for his beloved followers.*

Standing now in the middle of the upper room, Christ's first words were those of consolation. Condemning and scolding is not Christ's way. He appeared before his disciples despite locked doors—he was no longer hampered by any physical constraint. He walked through doors and walls; he appeared and disappeared here and there at will. And so in peace he came to the upper room and stood before a frightened crowd of disciples.

> *When it was evening on that day, the first day of the week, and the doors of the house where the disciples had met were locked for fear of the Jews, Jesus came and stood among them and said, "Peace be with you." (John 20:19)*

He brought a peace that cut through the darkness of fear. He understands the weakness of the human heart and desires to heal it, not berate it. He desires to heal the wounds of original sin that each of us bears in our heart. In a beautiful passage from St. Faustina's diary, the Lord says:

> *In the Old Covenant I sent prophets wielding thunderbolts to My people. Today I am sending you with My mercy to the people of the whole world. I do not want to punish aching mankind, but I desire to heal it, pressing it to My Merciful Heart. I use punishment when they themselves force Me to do so; My hand is reluctant to take hold of the sword of justice. Before the Day of Justice I am sending the Day of Mercy.*[2]

---

2 *Diary*, 1588.

The peace of Christ and his sweet presence filled the upper room much the way incense fills our churches. The next time you smell the incense at Mass, close your eyes for a moment and be aware that you are in the presence of Christ.

Christ knew the apostles were struggling to believe, so he showed them his hands and feet and side. He moved closer to each one of them, extending his hands in greeting and baring his wounds. He healed the wounds of the disciple's hearts by showing them his own wounds.

After he said this, he showed them his hands and his side. Then the disciples rejoiced when they saw the Lord. Jesus said to them again, "Peace be with you." (John 20:20–21)

By revealing his wounds Christ made himself "vulnerable" to his disciples. The passage tells us that they *rejoiced*. The eyes of the disciples first remained on the wounds, and then their eyes turned upward to look into the eyes of Christ—a brief beatific vision for each of them. Such a vision can only cause rejoicing!

Christ is the Crucified One who is risen and who bears his glorious wounds for all eternity. The disciple must become like the Master. *The process of becoming like Christ includes carrying the cross as Christ did and bearing wounds as Christ did.* By doing so the soul reaches the fullness of life and the eternal destiny to which it is called.

In the upper room Christ was so peaceful. He had the aura of eternity about him. He did not fret like a political organizer. He was not wielding a sword like a conqueror. He was not given to massive appearances and loud commotions about his person like a Hollywood star. And yet the world and all of history revolves around him.

Christ was not content to simply appear before the apostles. His passion and death had a purpose: to reveal God's love to mankind and open the doors to heaven for all. The Good News of his resurrection must now be shared. Our faith is not a personal gift to be hoarded. It is a gift to be given! And so his next words were a missionary mandate:

> *As the Father has sent me, so I send you. When he had said this, he breathed on them and said to them, "Receive the Holy Spirit. If you forgive the sins of any, they are forgiven them; if you retain the sins of any, they are retained." (John 20:21–23)*

Christ's missionary commandment must echo as strongly and urgently in the heart of every Christian as it did for those first apostles. Since the Christian vocation has love as its origin and objective, it is a call to love—it is a mission of love.

God the Father, moved by love, sent his Son into the world to save mankind. Christ in turn sent the apostles to the ends of the earth to preach the joyful news that God is love and the time of salvation has come.

The Church faces the permanent challenge of passing on this gospel to each new generation. Filled with Christ's charity, she too feels the urgency of fulfilling her missionary mandate to bring the gospel to every person, overcoming all the boundaries of time, culture, and place.

"My Lord and My God!"

Finally, a word must be said about Thomas, the doubting apostle. For some reason he was not present at the upper room at the time of the first appearance. He was destined to represent each one of us who could not be present at that moment. Down through the centuries millions of Christians will have the opportunity to believe as an "absent Thomas." It seemed like an unfortunate circumstance for Thomas that he stepped out and missed the Lord, yet it was actually a blessing in disguise.

Thomas was given the opportunity to be among the blessed who have not seen and yet believe. Unfortunately his faith was weak and he missed out on this blessing. However, each Christian since the Ascension can be part of this group and claim this blessing. We have not seen our Lord. We have only felt his love and heard his message as transmitted to us by a disciple. Our faith is both a gift and a blessing. In a way we are actually *more* blessed than the apostles who physically saw the Lord. Seeing and believing is not as precious to our Lord as faith without seeing.

Christ didn't reprimand Thomas or overly react to his weak faith. He understands the human heart. He created us as reasoning beings that are constantly in search of answers and in need of proof. On his return Our Lord appeared to Thomas and addressed him personally. He allowed Thomas to touch and see his wounds. When Thomas finally encountered the Risen Christ, he was overwhelmed by his grandeur and majesty. We tend to attach the title of "Doubting" to the name of Thomas, but we must remember that he also made the greatest proclamation of faith in the Bible. He calls Jesus "My Lord and My God!" Here Thomas directly called Jesus *God*, using a title that at first many were hesitant to use, as they were still trying to comprehend the mystery of the Father, Son, and Holy Spirit.

After Christ's ascension, the title of "Doubting Thomas" must have hurt Thomas deeply. It served as a constant reminder never to lose faith. Thomas would carry this wound in his heart for the rest of his life. However, Thomas' faith grew so large that he was granted the crown of martyrdom. He became a champion of the faith, proof that the gentle words of Christ to him that day were enough to heal and strengthen his wounded heart.

The upper room reveals a gentle and majestic Christ who heals broken hearts and joyfully sends out disciples bearing the greatest news. He comes, he calls, and he sends forth.

All of us at some time in our lives will experience the upper room of spiritual dryness. Our initial reaction to the cross may be, like that of the apostles, to run and hide. At God's approach we may be fearful like Adam and Eve who hid themselves at his approach. Our Lord, however, is always the Good Shepherd and won't rest until he finds us. He is aided by his Blessed Mother, who also seeks out the lost and weary children of God in order to bring them to her Son. During times of spiritual dryness, invite her into your upper room! Eventually, weary from your trials, you will encounter Christ who will strengthen you. Every difficulty in life, when turned over to Our Lord, becomes a beautiful cross to carry. Everything is an opportunity for grace; everything can be redemptive.

CHAPTER SIX

Christ on the Shore

The next place where we will encounter Christ is on the shore of the Sea of Galilee. This place marked the beginning of Peter's journey with the Lord. Christ passed along that shore one day, and Peter's life changed forever. A true encounter with Christ is always a transforming moment. We read:

> *Once while Jesus was standing beside the lake of Gennesaret, and the crowd was pressing in on him to hear the word of God, he saw two boats there at the shore of the lake; the fishermen had gone out of them and were washing their nets. He got into one of the boats, the one belonging to Simon, and asked him to put out a little way from the shore. Then he sat down and taught the crowds from the boat. (Luke 5:1–3)*

I entered the seminary on September 14, 1999. That night I received the Legionary cassock from my novice director at the Legion of Christ's novitiate in Connecticut. The tradition is to receive the black Roman cassock after night prayer on the eve of the Feast of Our Lady of Sorrows. We put on the cassock the next morning before going to the Mass. During the nighttime ceremony, the novice director reads a beautiful exhortation that motivates the new novice and asks that the uniform be worn faithfully and with dignity. As it was read that night, one of the lines really struck me: "Today Christ passes along the shore of your life!"

For all of us entering the novitiate in that moment, Christ had truly passed by the shore of our life and called out to us as he did to Peter and the sons of Zebedee. Up until that moment we had been living our own lives, making our own plans, seeking to make our dreams a reality. At a certain point Christ crossed our paths and from then on, just as for Peter and the apostles, our lives began to change. Our previous hopes and dreams slowly began to be the hopes and dreams of Christ. We no longer went about each day focused on ourselves and our human desires. We started asking what would please Christ, what desires were in his heart. As the seminary days went by, we became more centered on Christ and less centered on ourselves.

On the morning that forever changed the course of Peter's life, Christ was preaching to a large and growing crowd of people. He stood on the shore, just on the edge of the water. Slowly he was being pushed back toward the water by the multitude. Christ, as always, was a magnet for aching humanity. His words were spoken like fire, and the hearts of all who heard were burning.

Christ is keenly aware of his desire to call men and women to serve him and join him in the work of salvation. It was not by pure chance that Christ happened to be at the shore the day Peter was there tending his nets. Christ had prayed about this moment; he had thought of Peter as his first apostle. He went precisely where he knew Peter would be. Peter was unaware of what was about to happen. He had his mind on his work. Out of the corner of his eye, he saw the large group of people crowding around the rabbi from Nazareth. He continued with his work but listened nonetheless to the words of Christ. Somehow these words echoed in his soul. There was something very different about this rabbi.

Then Christ turned toward Peter. He needed his help in order to continue his mission. Christ again revealed his desire to allow each soul to follow him in complete freedom. He didn't command Peter to follow him. He only asked him for a little help. Christ wanted Peter to experience him first before deciding to follow him. Christ made a request of Peter—to use his fishing boat for a little while. He needed a place to preach where everyone could hear him. In the boat, just a few yards offshore, his voice would carry well and many more would be able to hear his message.

Peter agreed to the proposal. Peter took pride in his boat, and he might have been a little proud that Christ chose his boat among all the others. He would be able to grant the rabbi from Nazareth a platform to speak from, and all eyes would be directed toward his boat and he, as captain, would enjoy the moment. At the same time Peter was eager to hear more of these words. He may not have wanted to admit it at the moment, but he was hoping to spend more time near this teacher.

So Christ came onboard the boat and into Peter's life forever. Peter opened his heart just a little to Christ, and that was enough!

Christ now focused his attention on the people gathered on the shore. He continued to speak his merciful words about the Father's love. The day slowly moved on from the cool morning dawn to a bright, mid-morning sun. As Christ finished his preaching, he began his next mission. The entire time Our Lord had been preaching, more and more people had begun to line the shore. At the sight of these souls, so like sheep without a shepherd, the heart of Christ was moved with pity. Our Lord knew that, in the Father's plan, his days on earth were numbered. He knew that after his resurrection he would ascend to the right hand of the Father. Christ did not want to leave us orphans; in his place he planned to leave shepherds after his own heart. Peter would be the first shepherd, and after him a long line of shepherds would continue until the end of time. *Each and every vocation to the priesthood and consecrated life springs from this desire in the heart of Jesus to be present for all men in every age. These vocations have their source deep in the heart of Christ. They are made from Christ's love and sustained by his love in order to spread his love.* With this in mind, Our Lord turned toward Peter in his boat.

For Peter the boat represented many things. First it was his security. There in the boat Peter was in charge. He knew what to do and did it well. Life couldn't throw too many hard knocks at Peter while he was in his boat. There on the waves he felt secure.

The boat was also Peter's career path. Boats were not easy to build or to maintain in New Testament times. Peter's boat might have been handed down to him by his father. The boat was his source of income and his future well-being. It also represented a lot of work and effort. At the same time, as head of a fishing corporation, Peter had a social standing somewhat elevated from the rest of the common fishermen.

The boat represented Peter's heart. In the boat he made the plans; he called the shots. With hard and constant work, he would lack nothing. In his boat Peter was in a sense separated from the cares of the world. He was offshore and doing his own thing. He was a man whose main focus was himself and his immediate family. World events, such as Roman domination or the preaching of the Pharisees in the Temple never really interested him. They certainly concerned him, and he was aware of the difficulties of the times, yet Peter was on his own—a man for himself.

Yet for all the security and peace his boat could bring him, the boat was small. His hopes and dreams, however large, were never larger than what that little boat and little lake could provide. His human dreams lacked luster and adventure. They lacked a universal scope and an eternal horizon. This is what Christ wanted to change.

When a human makes plans without God, those plans are horizontal and limited, ultimately boring and commonplace. On the other hand, when we cooperate with God's plans, the story of our lives becomes eternal, exciting, and divine. Peter's life as just a fisherman without God would have been a forgotten life, routine and unworthy of note. Peter's life as an apostle was totally different.

Peter had many talents. He was a hard worker. He had an eye for finding the best time and place to fish. He had a lot of resilience and fortitude. Time and again he would throw the nets out and pull them up empty-handed. Yet he never gave up. He kept fishing. He had perseverance. Peter was also a capable manager—he directed the family fishing business. He was good with people; he had a familiarity with the market and prices and human interaction. Peter was also humble enough to be led, and Christ knew this. The human qualities that Peter possessed would prove to be very useful in his role as shepherd of the Church. Christ would elevate his human talent with divine grace. Simon Peter would slowly be molded into *Saint* Peter.

Christ addressed Peter again with another request.

When he had finished speaking, he said to Simon, "Put out into the deep water and let down your nets for a catch." Simon answered, "Master, we have worked all night long but have caught nothing. Yet if you say so, I will let down the nets." (Luke 5:4–7)

The future apostle did what Christ asked and was overwhelmed by the sudden emergence of a large school of fish, all swimming right into his nets. Peter called James and John to help him pull the nets into the boat. Just minutes before the boat had been empty. The work of Peter, James, and John had been fruitless. Now with Christ in the boat, everything changed. Their small worldview was shattered by the Divine Presence. Christ opened up a whole new world of possibilities.

Peter was stunned. His humble fisherman's life now seemed shallow and empty when faced with the person of Christ. His hard work and skills occasionally pulled in a few dozen fish, yet these skills were but a drop of water in the ocean of divine power. Peter knew he was a sinful man; he recognized his faults with humility. Faced with the divine, he revealed his poor humanity.

Peter's Jewish faith had taught him to fear God more than to love him—to follow the letter of the law but not the spirit. Peter had always kept a safe distance between himself and things divine. This rabbi from Nazareth, however, brought divinity right into Peter's boat—uncomfortably close. Now, stuck on a boat in the middle of the lake with nowhere to go, he knelt down amid the flopping fish.

He asked Christ to leave, to put again a safe distance between them. The gaze of Christ, which pierces to the heart, made Peter uncomfortable. Christ looked directly into his soul. After so many years of being in charge of his life and his boat, Peter was faced with the option of letting Christ direct things from now on. While it opened the horizons of his life to endless wonder and opportunities, it still meant forsaking the security of his boat. Peter says: "Go away from me, Lord, for I am a sinful man!" (Luke 5:8).

Peter bowed down before the divine majesty of Christ, with James and John standing behind him.

And Jesus said to them: "Come after me, and I will make you to become fishers of men." And immediately leaving their nets, they followed him. (Luke 5:11, Douay-Rheims)

Peter, James, and John left everything. Their simple lives as fisherman never had filled their hearts completely. Out on the lake, in the comfort of each other's presence, perhaps they had spoken of things divine. Perhaps they wondered together about eternity and God, about their faith and about the meaning of life. They were fisherman, but they might have become philosophers late at night out on the lake. Jesus, they sensed, somehow represented something lacking in their hearts. While their life as fishermen had given them security and moderate comforts, it was a horizontal existence and their hearts pined for something more. None of these three men were as of yet totally transformed into the courageous apostles we meet in the Book of Acts. They were slowly taking the first steps in their journey toward Christ. They sought a deeper meaning in life, and they knew they had a deeper calling.

I had a similar experience while studying during my senior year of high school at a minor seminary in New Hampshire. The school was located on a hill just above Lake Winnipesaukee. The beautiful lake stretched out twelve miles and provided an amazing view from the hilltop. It was the continual backdrop for all we did at the school.

I spent the summer that year discerning my vocation to the priesthood, and I certainly had many up-and-down moments. At times I was exuberant and enthusiastic about following Christ, and at other times, like Peter, I felt discouraged and afraid.

One day, however, I took a huge step forward in my understanding of the call to consecrate my life to the service of Christ the King. It happened during a morning reflection given by one of the Legionary priests who worked on the formation team at the school. It was late summertime, we had spent many hours over the previous weeks swimming and hiking along Lake Winnipesaukee. Just behind us through the chapel window, the whole length of the lake stretched out, revealing a beach frequented by many summertime vacationers.

The priest began speaking about the value of time and eternity. God gives all of us a certain amount of time on this earth. This time is a talent; what we do with it is up to us. We can live for ourselves, selfishly seeking our own pleasures and effectively burying this talent. Or we can live for others, trying to reach the end our time on earth with our arms full of good works of love, thus multiplying this talent.

When one thinks of life in this way, it makes sense that a man might give up his life to become a priest and work for the good of souls. It makes sense for a young woman to give up a family of her own to become a consecrated woman in order to touch the lives of thousands of souls by her spiritual motherhood. It also makes sense that one would enter into marriage seeking not one's own happiness but the happiness of one's spouse and future children.

The priest then invited us to look out the back window at the lakeshore. There were about a hundred people lying on blankets, sunning themselves, and cooling themselves off in the water. He continued by saying that there are people who spend their whole summer doing nothing else but cooling themselves off in the water. At the end of each day, they go home and say to themselves: "Ah, what a good day. I cooled myself off in the water!"

Their lives amount to nothing more than cooling themselves off in the water. When they die the Lord will ask them what they did with their life and time and they will have to say: "I cooled myself off in the water."

That didn't sound like what I would want to tell Christ on my judgment day!

There is nothing wrong with spending time relaxing. I'm sure there were many generous and good people on that beach taking a much-deserved vacation. The point is that many souls spend their entire lives doing very little else but seeking to make themselves as comfortable as possible. The amount of actual good works they do in life and the time they spend focused on others amounts to almost nothing in comparison to the years upon years they spend focusing only on themselves.

The priest concluded his talk by asking, "How do you want to spend your life?"

In that moment I knew that I wanted to spend my life working for the good of others. It wasn't specifically about my vocation to the priesthood—it was something deeper; it was about how I would live my life no matter where I ended up. Would the focus of my life be myself or others? As a priest I would be free to work full time doing good. If I were married, I would live my life centered on caring for my wife and children. *Hopefully, I thought, in whatever I end up doing, my lifetime on earth could be summed up in service to my brothers and sisters, and not in service to myself.*

When Peter brought his boat to shore and stepped out for the last time, he was stepping into eternity. From that moment his life changed from the monotonous throwing and pulling of nets into the sea in search of his own livelihood to seeking the livelihood of others. His life now embraced a nobler calling: He became a fisher of men. He would cast his nets out into the sea of humanity and bring in a multitude of souls for Christ. His work was no longer for himself; it was for God. His focus was not on himself but on souls. His horizons broke out of the limited dimensions of a little boat on a lake to the wide open horizons of an apostle. His life now meant something for eternity.

As Peter, James, and John walked away from the boat, their hearts became light and joyful. They were now free from attachments to things merely human. They experienced the peace of soul that so many Christians experience when their eyes are fixed on heaven. *The more cares we have for the things of this world, the heavier our hearts become as they are weighed down by attachments. Only Christ, the Man on the Shore, can free our hearts.* In your life, as each new day dawns, he stands before you on the shore. He beckons you to follow him, to run your boat aground and step onto the eternal shores. He calls you to join the ranks of men and women who have left everything to follow him.

He wishes to walk with you like he did with the disciples on the way to Emmaus. He will call you from your upper room. He wants to lead you to exotic and new lands as he did for St. John. He will always lead you in the direction of eternity.

PART TWO
THE GENTLE WAYS OF CHRIST

CHAPTER SEVEN

Christ and Women—Martha and Mary

Christ's journey took him to many different places in the Holy Land. He was always on the move, his heart burning with zeal to encounter more of his children. He rested little, prayed much, and loved much. He was the true Pilgrim, always aware that his homeland was elsewhere. He was a man who in his own words had "nowhere to lay his head" (Luke 9:58).

However, there was one place where our Lord could occasionally get a reprieve from his tiresome journeys and rest for a few days: Bethany, located two miles east of Jerusalem. The frequent Jewish festivals and the draw of the Temple itself often brought our Lord to Jerusalem. Christ had a special relationship with the Temple. It was a magnet for him; no doubt there he felt closer to his Heavenly Father. Christ knew he himself was the New Temple; the old Temple of Israel would pass away.

Given Bethany's close proximity to Jerusalem, it is safe to imagine Jesus having spent much time there. As with the Temple scenes, the house in Bethany could have also been a part of Jesus's early childhood. Archaeology has unearthed many ossuaries around Bethany with Galilean names, indicating that Bethany may have been a safe haven for Galilean pilgrims to Jerusalem. It is very possible that Bethany could have been a place where the Holy Family came to rest each year during Passover.

There were three siblings in Bethany with whom Jesus had a special relationship: Martha, Mary, and Lazarus. Perhaps Our Lord knew them from childhood. He obviously had a special love for them, not just because they invited him to stay in their home, but because their faith and simplicity were very welcoming to Christ.

Martha and Mary were two women of the early Church who experienced Christ in a personal and deep way. In this chapter we will especially focus on their hearts. Women by nature have the ability to love selflessly. They give life, nurture life, and support life. They know how to express love, give love, and receive love. Love is ever watchful; it feels no burden, has no limits, and sees everything as possible. At times, however, these hearts so capable of love can become difficult to manage. This watchfulness and limitlessness cannot come from a merely natural source. These hearts need a foundation beyond the merely human. Christ is this foundation. When a woman's heart is centered on Christ, there is peace and balance. Every human heart needs Christ. The stories of Martha and Mary teach us this.

Jesus felt very comfortable in the home of his good friends, simple generous folk all enjoying Martha's good cooking. He and his apostles no doubt spent many quiet and pleasant evenings around the table. There, in the home at Bethany, our Lord could allow himself to rest.

The three siblings in Bethany had quite different personalities. Martha and Mary were two unmarried sisters. Martha seems to be the older of the two; she always took charge, bustling about the home preparing this and that. Mary was contemplative and free-spirited; she spent time at the feet of the master, somewhat detached from the daily cares. And Lazarus was the man of the house, yet his attitude was one of service and humility. John referred to Lazarus as he whom Jesus truly loved (see John 11:3).

Our Lord loved the simple and humble, and no doubt this characterized Lazarus. Proof of his childlike simplicity is found in Martha being the one to run the house. And when Jesus arrived in Bethany, it was not Lazarus at the door but Martha. Martha knew that Christ was above the social mores of the time. He would allow a woman to welcome him into her home.

Lazarus was the man of the house, but he let Martha take the lead; it was *her* home. He was certainly a wealthy man, as evidenced by the expensive perfume found under his roof and his ability to play host to large groups of men. However, Lazarus was a hidden giver; Martha ran the house, and Mary was the one who presented the perfume to anoint Jesus, not Lazarus. Lazarus, living so near Jerusalem, surely spent many days a week in the temple area praying. When Jesus arrived, Lazarus sat with the Lord and listened to his words. No doubt they were very close.

These three siblings were each loved by Christ in a special way. Despite Martha's impulsiveness and distractions and Mary's aloofness and strong emotions, both women were souls of deep faith. When their brother was ill, both women sent immediately for Jesus, knowing he could heal him.

Welcoming the Lord

When Jesus arrived from a journey to Bethany, Martha greeted him at the door and began to act as hostess. Mary, on the other hand, had different plans.

A certain woman named Martha received him into her house. She had a sister named Mary, who sat at the Lord's feet and listened to what he was saying. (Luke 10:38–39)

Martha received the Lord, along with his twelve hungry apostles, into her home and quickly got down to work. Mary chose to remain with the Master.

We can imagine Martha looking around for her sister. In the dining room she hears the voice of Christ and the surrounding voices of his apostles and Lazarus. Where could Mary be? She checks the pantry, the back bedrooms, outside in the garden. Then she peeks into the dining area and sees Mary sitting in the middle of the room at the feet of the Master! Martha might have thought to herself: *There she goes again, throwing proper etiquette to the wind! She's sitting at the feet of Jesus, in the place of a disciple, in the middle of all the men!*

Mary's view toward the traditional roles of men and women was less strict than that of her sister. While Martha held fast to traditions, Mary's free-spirited nature led her beyond the norms, stretching them here and there to accommodate her vast spirit. Mary wouldn't let herself be pinned down under the cultural norms of her older sister, and this no doubt caused plenty of minor squabbles between the two sisters.

Martha waited for a break in the conversation in order to get close to Christ. In a moment when the group's attention was placed elsewhere, she slipped in next to Jesus, with a reproachful glance at Mary.

> *Martha was distracted by her many tasks; so she came to him and asked, "Lord, do you not care that my sister has left me to do all the work by myself? Tell her then to help me." (Luke 10:40)*

She never guessed that the Lord would not see her plight and take her side. He shocked her by saying:

> *"Martha, Martha, you are worried and distracted by many things; there is need of only one thing. Mary has chosen the better part, which will not be taken away from her." (Luke 10:41–42)*

Jesus contrasts Martha's distracted nature with Mary's focus. Martha had "many things" to worry about; Mary had the "one thing" and it was much better. Martha's intense worrying over the meal showed that her heart was in the wrong place. She was so wrapped up in the practical everyday things of the present moment that she forgot the reason behind all her work. She was not in the kitchen loving Christ amid the pots and pans; instead she was worried, anxious, thinking ill of Mary, and not at peace. *A heart where Christ is not the center is never at peace.*

On the other hand Mary's first priority was to spend time with Christ, not prepare a meal. She saw in Christ the ultimate reason for her life, without whom nothing made sense or had meaning. Her focus was God, and her soul was sensitive to the motions of the Spirit. In a beautiful way, she, unlike most of the people around Christ (save for the Blessed Mother and St. John the Evangelist), was aware of the moods and needs of Christ.

Christ's lesson served Martha well. The Gospel makes it clear that Jesus loved Martha very much. Her task-centered nature was not a problem, nor was her ability to run the house. It was her interior disposition and the motivations behind her daily efforts that Christ wanted to purify. Martha was not way off the mark, only slightly. But missing Christ by even a little meant that her heart would never be truly at peace. Her heart, though, was a heart of gold. So many poor people and weary travelers came to her door, and all found some sort of solace. Martha was always at work—it was the innocent joy of her life. Christ was allowing her heart to grow beyond the here and now and the hundreds of needy people around Bethany. Her heart now encompassed Christ and therefore all things.

Martha is symbolic of all active and laborious souls. They are the eternal organizers, the ones who have the capacity to see beyond the problems to the solution. As active types, they work to solve every problem that comes their way. Nothing is too hard to overcome. Many of you reading this can probably see yourselves depicted here in Martha. This is the quiet martyrdom of so many Catholic mothers who juggle running a house, caring for children, and even full-time jobs.

As seen with Martha, an active personality can bring about an obstacle to the spiritual life. I frequently come across many generous souls who try very hard to grow in holiness. They can list off all their spiritual works one by one: praying the Rosary each day, daily Mass, a few hours of Adoration during the week, morning and evening prayer, reading spiritual books and a daily reading of the Scriptures, parish work—the list goes on.

All of this is wonderful and laudable. However, a do-it-yourself, checklist-style of holiness doesn't work by itself in the spiritual life for one simple reason: *We are never the protagonists in our growth in holiness.* It is always the Holy Spirit, the Sanctifier who does the work in us. Our culture has a do-it-yourself approach to many things, but in the spiritual life there aren't any shortcuts. There aren't any "ten easy steps to holiness."

It is not the quantity of our spiritual work, but the quality. It is the love behind what we do that matters, not so much what we do. Many missionaries have gone off to faraway places to preach Christ, and that may seem like a sure sign of holiness. However, as St. Paul reminds us:

> *If I speak in the tongues of mortals and of angels, but do not have love, I am a noisy gong or a clanging cymbal. And if I have prophetic powers, and understand all mysteries and all knowledge, and if I have all faith, so as to remove mountains, but do not have love, I am nothing. (1 Corinthians 13:1–2)*

Whether you are off in the hills of Mexico as a missionary or cleaning the kitchen in a noisy home with children, in both cases you have the exact same opportunity to grow in holiness. One becomes a saint working hard and traveling to remote villages; the other becomes a saint amid the pots and pans of the everyday kitchen. *It is not what we do so much as why we do it—the focus and reason behind it.* If I wish to become a great painter, I can't just pour buckets and buckets of paint on a canvas and assume that by the sheer quantity of paint poured I will acquire the skills of painting. I need to take very little paint and lots of time practicing each day to acquire the skill of painting. The amount of quality I put into it will over time allow me to become a great painter. *It is the same in the spiritual life; many never become great saints because they never become great lovers.* They do endless good works or repeat many prayers, but because they don't grow in love, they are just pouring out buckets and buckets of paint. Instead of painting a picture, they just create a disordered mess.

Martha learned this lesson quickly, because the next time Christ came for dinner with his apostles, we hear no more complaints from her. Whether or not the Gospel of John presents a different scene is open to question, but most likely given the fact that John's Gospel places a visit by Christ to Bethany during Holy Week, we can assume the "Martha, Martha" scene happened on a previous visit. Given its special place in his heart, moments before the end of his life, when Christ was surely overburdened with many cares, he walked into the home at Bethany one last time. This time Lazarus greeted him with great affection, since shortly before Christ had raised him from the dead. Mary once again was at the feet of Christ.

Six days before the Passover Jesus came to Bethany, the home of Lazarus, whom he had raised from the dead. There they gave a dinner for him. Martha served, and Lazarus was one of those at the table with him. (John 12:1–2)

Martha again was busy serving. This was her place; she loved doing it. This time, however, it was out of total love. She found God amid the daily chores of her life and was now painting a beautiful picture of holiness. Her heart was at peace, even though Mary was once again at the feet of Jesus and she was alone serving.

True growth in holiness does not always mean changing what we do; sometimes it's changing *why* we do it. Growing in holiness is a daily renewing of our commitment to Christ, a purifying of our hearts.

Loving the Lord with Abandon

Let us turn our attention to Mary now. She was much different than her sister. Mary was a woman who sought a deep love. She realized that no earthly thing would ever fill her heart completely. Her heart was too big and her spirit desired to touch the whole world in one embrace. Her life was full of good works, and she most likely accompanied Lazarus into Jerusalem to be near the Temple as much as she could.

Perhaps her heart had wandered far and wide before she found Christ. Her resistance to follow the footsteps of her older sister could have started in childhood. Her behavior at the death of her brother also showed a sort of spontaneous abandonment of self. She wailed and wept and was given to spontaneous bursts of lamentation. The people in her household thought nothing of it when she suddenly stood up and ran out the door. Just Mary being Mary…

I won't ponder too much on where her temperament and free-spirited nature could have led her in her early years. Let it suffice to say that her carefree heart and relaxed social mores were certainly a risky mix.

Finally, however, when Christ entered her life, she found completeness. She found true freedom; she was free because her heart was free. Her heart had one attachment: Christ. The Lord perfected her heart. The wide horizons and possibilities that filled her heart were not stifled when Christ came; instead they were focused. Mary had the "one thing" necessary.

And like Martha, when Christ came into her home, she had no need to change *what* she did—just *why* she did it.

As a symbol of her growth in love and the focusing of her heart on Christ alone, John related the story of Jesus's anointing by Mary. Mary took some precious and very costly perfume from a back room. Without words she poured it upon Christ's feet and used her hair to dry them. Her actions were beyond words. When a soul truly loves Christ, no words are necessary. Love can be communicated without words. After this kind act, Judas speaks up.

"Why was this perfume not sold for three hundred denarii and the money given to the poor?" He said this not because he cared about the poor, but because he was a thief; he kept the common purse and used to steal what was put into it. Jesus said, "Leave her alone. She bought it so that she might keep it for the day of my burial. You always have the poor with you, but you do not always have me." (John 12:5–8)

John treated Judas severely in his Gospel, always linked to his betrayal. Judas's words about the poor are understood best in Bethany, where a poorhouse was located. Jesus more gently makes reference to the poorhouse, when he notes that the poor are always nearby. Judas's heart was the opposite of Mary's. His heart was not free—it was cold and calculating, manipulative and dark. In Mary's heart there were no attachments to anything else but Christ. She sacrificed the best she had. Mary was, because of her great and pure love for Christ, a generous and noble soul.

Christ loved Bethany because he could physically rest there, and he could rest spiritually in the hearts of the three siblings. The stories of Martha and Mary reveal Jesus's deep appreciation for the feminine genius. The two women in Bethany teach all Christians the lesson that one experiences deep peace when one's heart becomes another Bethany for Christ. A pure heart that seeks to love, not harboring grudges or ill thoughts, a heart that is simple and kind, is a heart where Jesus can dwell.

CHAPTER EIGHT

Christ and Women—The Village of Magdala

Christ's dealings with women broke with the common practice of the times. While in most places women had a lower status than men and were often treated as possessions, Christ's ways were entirely different. His dealings with women were refreshing, novel, and beautiful. He saw women for who they truly are: daughters of God. He was not confined to the social mores of the time, always thinking and doing exactly as he pleased. For Christ, to live was to love. He was who he was, always and everywhere. Women were his mothers and sisters and daughters. He spoke to them, approached them, praised them, healed them, and loved them. In this chapter we will look at a beautiful encounter Jesus had with a woman who had suffered for many years.

One day Jesus was on the shore of the Sea of Galilee in the territory of the Gerasenes. Outside the village there was a cave where a man had been dwelling. He was possessed by an evil spirit and therefore unable to live in society. A complete outcast, he was left to wander the deserted places. Precisely there, all alone on his "exotic island," this pitiable man found Christ. When Christ encountered him he expelled the demons and sent the man on his way. Some nearby villagers arrived on the scene, overtaken by fear. Somehow, whatever miracles this man called Jesus of Nazareth was doing were too dangerous and frightening for them. They decided amongst themselves to send him away. They actually told God he was not welcome!

If they only knew what they had just done! They had almost had the privilege of having God himself come to their village for the evening. He would have dined in their houses and blessed their children. But an unholy fear of the Lord kept Christ at a distance. They were afraid of change, afraid of the unknown. They did not embrace the exciting adventure of following Christ.

Christ obliged the villagers. He was a gracious and generous spirit, going where he was welcomed and not forcing himself on anyone. So he got into a boat and proceeded to the other side of the lake. There he encountered the woman who had been ill and suffering for many years.

From the shore of the Gerasenes, the town of Magdala lies naturally opposite the shore and is therefore the "other side of the lake" to which Jesus crossed. It is the town where Mary Magdalene lived. Recent excavations of Magdala confirm this.

On this site, excavating began in earnest when the remains of an uncommonly large synagogue were unearthed during the initial pre-building investigation. Of the many things found in the ruins of Magdala, the most notable to date are a first-century synagogue, a home for the chief rabbi, a fish market, and a table altar for placing the Torah. The decorations on this altar contain the oldest image of a menorah to date.

This unearthed synagogue dates back to the time of Jesus, so we can assume that Jesus visited there many times.

Jesus went throughout Galilee, teaching in their synagogues and proclaiming the good news of the kingdom and curing every disease and every sickness among the people. (Matthew 4:23)

In fact, the excavations match perfectly the description in the Gospels of the following account. We read:

When Jesus had crossed again in the boat to the other side, a great crowd gathered around him; and he was by the sea. Then one of the leaders of the synagogue named Jairus came and, when he saw him, fell at his feet and begged him repeatedly, "My little daughter is at the point of death. Come and lay your hands on her, so that she may be made well, and live." (Mark 5:21–23)

The place where Christ disembarked was the marketplace, bustling with people—hence the "large crowd" that gathered around him. Christ is always and everywhere a magnet for mankind, and on this account he encountered a man named Jairus.

Jairus was the president of the synagogue, a title that meant more than a rabbi; he was a type of arch-rabbi. Thus Jairus was an important man, known by everyone in the village. As he approached Jesus the crowd parted, opening up a way for him. He was naturally given the first opportunity to speak to Christ. Within the earshot of all, Jairus made a public act of faith in this new rabbi from Nazareth.

Jairus risked his career and reputation. Before all the men of the town, Jairus fell at the feet of Christ. He didn't maintain an air of importance. He didn't whisper his need quietly to Christ; he didn't care what anyone else thought of him. For Jairus what was important was not his fame or reputation or career—it was his daughter. Nothing else entered into this devoted father's mind. He is a model for all fathers.

Christ was pleased with the man's faith. He knew that Jairus's heart was authentic and sincere. Christ loves dealing with souls that are simple, humble, and trusting. They are easily carried in his Sacred Heart, easily transformed by grace. They are childlike. So Christ obliged Jairus and walked with him to his home. Jairus brought Christ into his home. This is the father's role: to welcome Christ into the family, unafraid of what the neighbors might think.

CHRIST'S HEALING TOUCH

A large crowd followed them. The first woman we want to focus on now made her appearance. We read:

> *Now there was a woman who had been suffering from hemorrhages for twelve years. She had endured much under many physicians, and had spent all that she had; and she was no better, but rather grew worse. She had heard about Jesus, and came up behind him in the crowd and touched his cloak, for she said, "If I but touch his clothes, I will be made well." (Mark 5:25–28)*

The woman was suffering from a very difficult illness. Over a decade of doctors and treatments had left her wiped out, financially ruined, and even sicker. She had been on an emotional roller coaster for twelve years. Each new doctor increased her hopes for healing. She spent more money, hoped and prayed, and for a few weeks she would feel better. But then the inevitable happened—the illness persisted and she sunk more deeply into her own despair and pain. This cycle had repeated itself over and over.

One day she heard about this Jesus who was known to be a healer. He preached God's mercy and love. He was a man who possibly could save her from her affliction. Despite her heart warning her not to get her hopes up, she couldn't resist Christ. Just as Jairus had been drawn to Christ, so was she. She approached, however, incognito. She came from behind, barely daring to touch him at all. She had given up any hope of treatment, of solving her problems by her own skill or talents. She now placed her hopes and fears in the hands of Christ. She had no more human means to solve her problems. Christ was her last hope.

She fearfully approached behind Christ and worked her way through the crowd, her veil tight over her bowed head. She focused on Christ and inched closer until she managed to get right behind him. She reached out and touched his cloak. She didn't reach out for medicines; she reached out in faith and merely touched Christ. Her faith was what healed her, not her own talents.

> *Immediately her hemorrhage stopped; and she felt in her body that she was healed of her disease. Immediately aware that power had gone forth from him, Jesus turned about in the crowd and said, "Who touched my clothes?" (Mark 5:29–30)*

When we walk through a crowd of people, we are among strangers, an impersonal group. But Christ never sees a crowd—he sees each and every one individually. He knows every person's heartbeat and their every desire and need.

Jesus knew completely the plight of this woman. He understood that she would only approach him from behind. Her fear and trembling left her unable to stand up in the crowd as Jairus had done. The Gerasenes had an unholy fear of the Lord. They feared Christ and so sent him away. *The woman in Magdala feared Christ, too, but the Holy Spirit gave her a true fear of the Lord. This holy fear actually drew her toward Christ.* In her humility and weakness, she sought a quiet, backdoor way of coming to Christ. The merciful heart of Christ obliged. He becomes all things to all men. He knows the way to deal with each soul, treating each one according to their needs. Just as no two saints are alike, no two human beings will every have the same relationship with Christ—each one is unique and beautiful. Jairus had a head-on encounter with Christ; this woman has a quiet behind the scenes encounter. Christ appeared to turn his back on the woman, but he knew full well that in doing so, he was actually turning toward her.

This story teaches us that suffering, when offered up in love, brings us closer to Christ. It becomes a union with Christ on the cross. Our Lord told St. Faustina:

My child, you please Me most by suffering. In your physical as well as your mental sufferings, My daughter, do not seek sympathy from creatures. I want the fragrance of your suffering to be pure and unadulterated. I want you to detach yourself, not only from creatures, but also from yourself. My daughter, I want to delight in the love of your heart, a pure love, virginal, unblemished, untarnished. The more you will come to love suffering, My daughter, the purer your love for Me will be.[1]

Christ broke through the darkness of this woman's life in a way no one in her time and culture believed possible. This woman had suffered physically for twelve painful years. However her physical sufferings were nothing compared to her moral trials. Her Jewish faith told her that sickness was the result of sin. She saw her twelve years of pain as twelve years of punishment from God. She did not see herself as a daughter of God, nor did she understand that God could love her. She held herself unworthy and imperfect, flawed somehow. Though she had no grave sins, nothing to merit divine punishment, for some reason she was being punished, and that was that. If you asked her if God loved her, she would have said he couldn't possibly love someone like her. If you asked her to describe who God was, she would have described a judge, a lawgiver—a fierce and just God with an iron fist who kept his distance from people like her.

Her experience of Christ was spiritually and physically life-changing. She hoped in Christ and was cured. Christ called her, giving her the opportunity to acknowledge him before men, to stand up and shake off her doubts and fears. This public moment for her was also a healing moment. The crowd knew of her—she was the sick woman who must have sinned gravely. The

---

1 *Diary*, 279.

gossip about her was well known. So Christ also lifted her up before the crowd, showing them the beauty of a soul that trusts in God. He taught the crowd that, while in their minds this woman among them was cursed and punished, in reality she was most blessed because of her faith. In the temple he did the same thing when he praised the poor widow's offering. What was small in the eyes of men is great in the eyes of God. *Truth and reality are found only in God's eyes. As God sees you, that is how you truly are.* The judgments of men are nothing but appearances.

> *But the woman, knowing what had happened to her, came in fear and trembling, fell down before him, and told him the whole truth. He said to her, "Daughter, your faith has made you well; go in peace, and be healed of your disease." (Mark 5:33–34)*

Christ revealed to her in a single word who God truly was. He banished forever in her mind the idea of an angry God. Christ, in his full divinity, called her "daughter." In her heart she now knew the one and only truth we all must learn: God is Father.

The words "my daughter" were the most beautiful words she had ever heard. As she had been physically healed by touching Christ, she now was healed emotionally and spiritually by listening to his words. This inner healing was more important. Physical wellness is nothing—eternal life is everything. Christ said it is better to enter life lame than to enter the eternal fires whole. Even today many souls are healed by the silent prayer of Eucharistic Adoration. There, before the Lord, listening to his soothing voice, he heals interiorly.

But the story does not end there. We will meet the second woman when Jesus continues on to the home of Jairus.

RESTORED TO LIFE

While on the way a messenger announced to Jairus that his daughter had died. Imagine the pain of that moment for Jairus! We've already seen that his life was centered on his family and his beloved daughter. She was the reason he did so many things in life, and without her his world came crashing down. Her death brought an emptiness to his life that only Christ will be able to fill. Jairus was silent in his grief, but in his most desperate hour he continued to trust in Christ. Together they continued on to Jairus's home.

Christ entered into the room where the daughter of Jairus lay dead. In a miraculous yet simple way, our Lord restored her to life. As she opened her eyes, imagine what she saw first: the eyes of Christ, the face of God himself! Here was proof of God's love, of God's presence on the earth.

Next she looked directly behind Christ to the loving face of her father in tears. In that moment the gratitude she had toward her human father must have been beyond expression. Her human father brought Christ to her; he was willing to risk everything for her. How many daughters today would benefit from a father who would love them unconditionally, who would bring Christ into their lives, who would live for others, not just for themselves and their hobbies.

The woman with the hemorrhage and the daughter of Jairus experienced Christ and were made whole. One was seen as a sinner, a burden on society. The other was seen as beyond help, dead and soon to be forgotten. Many a faithful Christian woman sees herself as beyond help, as imperfect and unworthy of God's love. They look into the mirror and don't like what they see. However, this passage from the Gospel proclaims a beautiful truth. While we may not like what we see, God himself does. God's eyes see us as we truly are, and he longs for each one of us to come to realize this truth.

How does Christ see women? He sees beloved daughters, and that is all that matters.

CHAPTER NINE

Christ and Men—Peter on the Shore

In an earlier chapter we left Peter standing on the shore about to begin his journey with Christ. Let's pick up his story three years later. Peter had been formed by Christ little by little into the leader of the apostolic band. Christ had died and risen from the dead, but he had not yet ascended. He appeared here and there to his disciples, and in this beautiful scene found in John 21, Christ once again passed by the shore of Peter's life.

The first time Christ called Peter to the shore, it was to begin his personal transformation from Simon Peter the fisherman to Peter the disciple. In this second calling, Peter was transformed into Peter the Shepherd of the Church.

Peter suffered a tremendous blow to his confidence when he denied Jesus three times. Now, a week or so after the Resurrection, Peter was still suffering. It was an interior wound that caused him to withdraw into himself. This is how most men tend to suffer—they go into themselves, brooding over a particular wound and suffering over and over, reliving the tragic moment. Peter retreated into what today we would call his "man cave": his boat, anchored safely offshore.

Peter gained solace from being out there on the water. It was exactly there on the lake that he first had been called by Christ. That was where his vocation began. By revisiting that site, he gained strength. *One thing was clear for Peter: Christ had called him. Christ knew his weakness and his frailty, and despite this knowledge, he still called him.* Peter was strengthened by this thought, knowing that even if he fell spiritually, as long as he picked himself up all would be set right. Christ knows our weaknesses, yet he still calls us. *It doesn't matter in the end how many times you fall down, as long as you allow Christ to pick you up again.*

Christ desired to reveal himself again to the apostles, and so he sought them out. He knew just as he did three years ago exactly where to find Peter: there in his boat out on the lake. Christ comes to the shore and calls Peter again.

> *After these things Jesus showed himself again to the disciples by the Sea of Tiberias; and he showed himself in this way. Gathered there together were Simon Peter, Thomas called the Twin, Nathanael of Cana in Galilee, the sons of Zebedee, and two others of his disciples. Simon Peter said to them, "I am going fishing." They said to him, "We will go with you." They went out and got into the boat, but that night they caught nothing. (John 21:1–4)*

Peter was always the leader. He said he was going to fish, and all those around him immediately joined in. They all knew that Peter had been chosen by Christ to be the leader in his absence. Even if they didn't enjoy fishing, they weren't going to leave Peter to do it alone. So they faithfully joined him. One can imagine the jokes between them about Peter's fishing skills. All night they caught nothing; this had happened to Peter before.

But Peter was not so much fishing as contemplating. He couldn't shake the memory of that fateful night, Holy Thursday. He had failed Christ just moments after swearing total fidelity to him. He can't be at peace with it; it was eating him up inside. The best way he knew to distract himself was fishing. He sat in the boat, in the darkness.

Peter and his companions caught nothing. They were in the boat, in the dark, without Christ. If Christ is not in the boat, one catches nothing. All that was about to change, however. Just after daybreak, when the light of the sun was becoming visible, Christ came and revealed his glory. Christ always brings light. Where Christ is, there is no darkness. In that moment—as on the road to Emmaus—Christ was unrecognizable to the apostles. Jesus was in his resurrection glory and his appearance had changed.

Jesus said to them, "Children, you have no fish, have you?" They answered him, "No." He said to them, "Cast the net to the right side of the boat, and you will find some." (John 21:5–6)

Christ always has a solution for every problem, yet he doesn't force us to use his solutions. He simply comes as a guest and offers help. He didn't scold the apostles for not having any fish, or for trying to fish without him; instead he accompanied them in their lives without force. He waited to be accepted.

After a weary night of fishing, the apostles were too tired to think much about the command of the stranger on the beach. They cast the nets, and in so doing the moment seemed strangely familiar. Slowly it dawned on them that this had happened before!

So they cast it, and now they were not able to haul it in because there were so many fish. That disciple whom Jesus loved said to Peter, "It is the Lord!" (John 21:6–7)

John was the first to recognize the Lord. Those who are pure of heart, as the Beatitudes say, are able to see God. John, young and pure in heart, was able to penetrate each situation and see the hand of God. Thus, of all the disciples in the boat, John recognized the Master first. He quickly made a correlation between this miracle of fish and the miracle of fish previously made by Christ. Only Christ could perform such wonders!

John told Peter that the Lord was on the beach. It hit Peter like a bolt of lightning and took his breath away. Again his Master was there, the Master he betrayed. Peter, always impulsive, just dove into the water, eager to cross the distance that divided them. He threw himself into the water instead of trying to walk this time. He swam, he allowed himself to sink; he no longer deemed himself worthy to walk on the water with Christ. His pride has been broken—his rejection of Christ has made him humble. He ducked under the water, kicking and pulling himself toward Christ.

The last time this scene happened, he brought his boat to shore and then stepped out with Christ; this time he abandoned his boat on the lake. He won't bring it in again so as to later go out. Peter had finally burned his ship and left all attachments behind.

This was now the second time Peter found himself on the water separated from Christ.

But the other disciples came in the boat, dragging the net full of fish, for they were not far from the land, only about a hundred yards off. When they had gone ashore, they saw a charcoal fire there, with fish on it, and bread. (John 21:8–9)

Peter arrived at the shore before the other apostles and stood dripping before Christ. Peter was nervous—he could barely bring himself to look Christ in the eye. This was the first time he was alone with Christ since his denial, and he wasn't sure what to say. Thankfully the arrival of the boat and the fish gave him something to do and provided a welcome distraction.

As men who are nervous and preoccupied with a problem tend to do, Peter distracted himself with activity. He wanted to serve the Master, to help him in any way. Christ was aware of the deep spiritual wound in Peter's heart that needed healing. Christ, in his gentle way, knew Peter well and knew exactly how to heal him.

Christ was already cooking some fish and bread over a charcoal fire, but he asked for more fish.

So Simon Peter went aboard and hauled the net ashore, full of large fish, a hundred fifty-three of them; and though there were so many, the net was not torn. Jesus said to them, "Come and have breakfast." Now none of the disciples dared to ask him, "Who are you?" because they knew it was the Lord. Jesus came and took the bread and gave it to them, and did the same with the fish. (John 21:11–13)

The apostles were hungry and cold from their work the night before. They needed food and warmth. Christ, the master of humanity, knew exactly what they needed. But even more than the food and warmth, the apostles needed Christ's presence. They didn't speak; they just enjoyed the moment. They had stepped out of time into eternity—which is Christ.

Christ was preparing Peter as well. He knew Peter wanted to see him and speak with him personally and make amends for his denial. Peter's heart was broken, and Christ the Divine Doctor was now about to heal it. So he took Peter for a walk, apart from the other apostles and out of earshot.

He walked along the lakeshore with Peter. This second walk together on the shore was a moment of deeper transformation for Peter.

The way Christ dealt with Peter is worth reflecting on. Peter was a soul in distress. As a priest I encounter these souls every day. They enter the church, many times sitting in the back pews. They are afraid of revealing their hearts and wounds. Through the prayers of many faithful souls, the wounded sons and daughters of God eventually make their way to the confessional. When

I encounter souls so bruised and broken, my words are always mercy and peace. Space must be given for the soul to encounter Christ.

While at times from the pulpit sins must be vigorously attacked, the way to deal with each person individually is the way of Christ. Christ is never abrupt, never scolding or making public reprimands. He doesn't belittle anyone or use sarcasm. In my short time as a priest, I have too often encountered souls who have long been away from the Church for one reason: A priest belittled them and scolded them and humiliated them in the confessional. Maybe that was the style in years past, but it has never been the way of Christ. He took Peter for a walk, walking by his side, knowing it would be easier for Peter to not have to look him directly in the eye. Peter had already done that at the Last Supper when he vowed to Christ that he would never fail him.

When they had finished breakfast, Jesus said to Simon Peter, "Simon, son of John, do you love me more than these?" He said to him, "Yes, Lord; you know that I love you." Jesus said to him, "Feed my lambs." (John 21:15)

Christ gave Peter a chance to speak. He gave him his space and through his question opened a dialogue with Peter. Peter was not as good with words as he was with actions. He struggled to find the words he longed to say. He affirmed his love for Christ and then fell silent again. He pondered Christ's command to "Feed my lambs." Peter knew he was not worthy—he had failed Christ too many times.

They walked for a little while longer in silence, and then the Lord surprised him with a second question, the same as the first.

A second time he said to him, "Simon son of John, do you love me?" He said to him, "Yes, Lord; you know that I love you." Jesus said to him, "Tend my sheep." (John 21:16)

They now advanced down the shore a bit, and Peter was feeling a little more at ease. The walk and being able to twice affirm his love for Christ put Peter at peace. Our Lord, however, approached the issue that weighed so heavily on Peter. By asking him a third time, "Do you love me?" he drew a direct link to Peter's threefold denial. This pained Peter because Christ put his finger directly on the wound that required healing.

Christ was delicate and merciful, but he didn't skirt the issues. Our souls need to confront our wounds—to accept our own misery and accept the mercy of Christ. So Christ asked Peter this third question.

He said to him the third time, "Simon son of John, do you love me?" Peter felt hurt because he said to him the third time, "Do you love me?" And he said to him, "Lord, you know everything; you know that I love you" (John 21:17).

Peter now poured his heart out. The pain of his threefold denial was healed by his threefold affirmation. Yet he had no words to describe what was in his heart. Peter needed to simply turn to the Lord and beg his understanding. "Lord, you know me! You know my heart!"

This was the prayer Peter made to Our Lord. It was unformulated and spontaneous, yet it was deep and beautiful. Christ consented and said:

> *"Feed my sheep. Very truly, I tell you, when you were younger, you used to fasten your own belt and to go wherever you wished. But when you grow old, you will stretch out your hands, and someone else will fasten a belt around you and take you where you do not wish to go." He said this to indicate the kind of death by which he would glorify God. After this he said to him, "Follow me." (John 21:17–19)*

Christ restored Peter's dignity, accepted his repentance, and poured out his grace. Yet Christ told Peter that, in spite of all Christ's grace, Peter would still suffer the cross. Peter had a personality that did not readily accept the cross and suffering. Peter would always suffer, but from now on his suffering would be redemptive.

Once again, on the same shore, in the same place, Christ renewed his call to Peter: "Follow me!" Christ will always renew that call to his chosen ones. A priest who in weakness falls into sin can always be restored by God's grace. A failing marriage can be healed by Christ's love. A consecrated woman who lets her heart wander will be strengthened in her vocation by one look at Christ. Our Lord is full of forgiveness and understanding and mercy. Simply turn to Christ and you will hear once again the words that moved your heart in the past: "Come, follow me!"

Peter was restored, and once again he assumed his role as shepherd of the Church, caring for the flock of Christ. He turned and saw John, a person he knew was close to the Lord. He thought of John's future—what would become of him?

> *Peter turned and saw the disciple whom Jesus loved following them; he was the one who had reclined next to Jesus at the supper and had said, "Lord, who is it that is going to betray you?" When Peter saw him, he said to Jesus, "Lord, what about him?" Jesus said to him, "If it is my will that he remain until I come, what is that to you? Follow me!" (John 21:20–22)*

John's martyrdom was the slow passing of many years before he was able to be with Christ again. Peter's martyrdom was suffering a death like his Lord's. Both had great merit. John finished the narrative for us when he said:

> *This is the disciple who is testifying to these things and has written them, and we know that his testimony is true. But there are also many other*

things that Jesus did; if every one of them were written down, I suppose
that the world itself could not contain the books that would be written.
(John 21:24–25)

Christ's dealing with men is always unique and personal. He is always peaceful, but he is also direct, accomplishing his work. Going to Christ as Peter did, in your weakness, will be without a doubt the most beautiful event of your life. In baptism you entered into divine life as a son of God. When Christ called you, he crossed your path and entered into your adult life. Both are moments to cherish. And when you fall, return to him and hear his words again: "Come, follow me!"

As John said, many of the miracles and actions of Christ, no less important, were not written in the Gospels. They are, however, written on the hearts of men. Each one of you reading this book has an experience of Christ written in the living book of your life. What does your story say? How would you write it?

CHAPTER TEN

Christ and Children—"Let Them Come to Me"

Christ has a tender spot in his heart for children. Their purity and simplicity allows him to welcome them totally into his arms and into his heart. During his time on earth, the children, with their innocent faces, deep trust, and simple faith, reminded him of his heavenly kingdom. Our Lord taught us that the kingdom of heaven belongs to the childlike. When he was close to the little children, Christ felt close to his Father.

In his preaching, Christ extolled and defended the little ones, and he praised any adult who lives with simplicity and love as they do. Souls like Lazarus—who don't complicate their lives with human mistrust and reasoning, but allow God to always have his rightful place in their lives—are truly childlike. Christ constantly called his disciples to become "childlike" and "simple as doves."

After a few missionary trips to Haiti, I came to understand better this love of Christ for the little children. Haitian children have a hard life. The earthquake left the already impoverished country in stark misery. Most of the children have little chance to receive an education. In places such as Port-au-Prince, their food is mostly beans and rice imported by the United Nations relief agencies. In some parts, employment is only at 5 percent. So the future is bleak. However where the children suffer the most, Christ is ever more present.

Christ continually called the little children to him. We read: "Then little children were being brought to him in order that he might lay his hands on them and pray" (Matthew 19:13).

I am always touched when a parent approaches me with their child and asks for a blessing. I really sense that, in that moment, I am continuing the mission of Christ and allowing myself to be his hands and feet. Haitians in particular love blessings, and so I spend quite a bit of time blessing people while I am there. One Easter the Missionaries of Charity asked me to hand out bags of candy and food to all the people after Easter Sunday Mass. There were at least 600 people at Mass, and all of them wanted a blessing along with the gift bag. Six hundred blessings later, I was tired, but it was a beautiful day—truly a day of the Lord.

At a clinic in Port-au-Prince, one of our missionaries, a premed student from Chicago, was praying the Chaplet of Divine Mercy next to the bedside of a very sick baby. She was there for a while, and I was touched by her dedication to prayer and her hope for saving the baby's life. As she finished praying and was about to leave for another room in the orphanage, a Haitian mother at a nearby crib stopped her. Taking her hand she brought the missionary over to the crib of her own baby and making signs and gestures made it known that she deeply desired the missionary to pray over her child as well.

The missionary was so touched by this that she was moved to tears, and she began to pray the chaplet over again, this time at the crib of this poor child. Later that day the missionary told me the story and how much it had impacted her. For a moment she, the missionary, was truly taking Christ's place.

Six months after my ordination to the priesthood, when I was in Haiti for the first time, I had a very beautiful experience. I was just getting the hang of my priestly ministries and was settling into life as a young priest. Haiti was a big test for me. I knew I would be called upon to do bedside ministry, care for the sick and dying, and console the grieving. There is only so much one can learn in seminary; a lot has to be learned by jumping into it, sink or swim.

A CULTURE OF VOODOO

Little did I know that one of the most beautiful events of my life would take place on this mission trip. Before I tell the story, I must explain a little bit about an unfortunate element of Haiti: voodoo. There are strong undercurrents of voodoo mixed in with the culture. In some ways it is considered a national pastime. Even while walking through the airport, there are art murals depicting Haitians engaged in voodoo rituals. Much of it is due to a lack of instruction in the faith. Ultimately voodoo is diabolic.

It was June, the month dedicated to the Sacred Heart of Jesus, and we were enthroning images of the Sacred Heart in the tents the people lived in. I was walking through the tent city wearing my priestly stole. Twice people reacted strangely upon seeing the sisters, a few missionaries, and me coming down the road. Some ran off screaming, while others bolted into their tents. One woman stared at us for a while before yelling something in Creole I didn't understand. The sisters tried to get into one tent so that I could bless it and enthrone the image of the Sacred Heart, but the inhabitants would have nothing to do with us. The sisters murmured between themselves something about voodoo before we pressed on.

Later one little girl was brought into the clinic and left there by her mother. The child screamed and yelled and was hysterical. Her eyes were wide open and she was clawing and twisting while trying to climb up out of the crib and onto a windowsill. The sister in charge was visibly worried, but she took it in stride. She told me nonchalantly, "In the house of this little girl, objects move around and many other strange things happen. Someone is very much into voodoo in her home."

The little girl would not let us touch her or hold her. Sister filled a tub with holy water and bathed the little girl in it. Quickly she became subdued and turned into a frightened little lamb. Her eyes were still wide open, but now she was calm and worn out. I gave her a blessing and held her for a while, amazed at the radical change that came over her. Over the next few days, all of us took turns holding little Mesmerelda who was slowly becoming a normal little girl. Unfortunately the girl had to return to her home after a few weeks.

At other times the mothers brought their babies into the clinic with amulets and charms around their necks and wrists. The sisters patiently cut the objects off, threw them into the trash, and burned them. They explained to the mothers in firm words that the charms were evil.

The orphanage always presented a heartwrenching site. Almost one hundred babies filled an equal number of cribs. The few sisters and hired women in the orphanage busily tried to attend to them all, but they were always stretched very thin and needed a lot more help. After the earthquake a large number of the children in the clinic were orphans, and the rest were sick babies that mothers from the tent city brought in for treatment.

On that first trip after my ordination, when I first entered the children's home with a group of missionaries, I saw some of the babies standing up in their cribs, others sitting, and many on their backs—but all had their heads turned toward the door. They were whimpering and sad, looking at each missionary who walked in. They reached up toward us with outstretched arms. They wanted to be held and loved.

We scooped up as many babies as we could and started feeding, clothing, and changing their diapers as fast as we could. It was a dream come true for many of the missionaries—they loved children and could have spent hours working there.

I tried to pick up the first boy I saw. Something was wrong because, unlike every other baby, he was curled up in his crib and turned away from the door. Every other baby was reaching out through the bars of the cribs and calling out to be held. One of these babies was not like the others!

I tried to pick him up, but he pulled away and tensed up. He made a growling sound and moaned, making it clear he did not want to be held. At first I didn't think much of it, and I turned to the next crib where a toddler named Demitry was hopping up and down, reaching out to me to pick him up. He was a thin little guy, obviously underfed. He was sucking on two of his little fingers, so much so that he was wearing away the skin. As I held Demitry I sort of forgot about the boy in the corner.

A few hours later I again noticed the boy in the corner. Two of the missionaries were talking about him and both said they had the same experience—they had tried to pick him up, but he pulled away. I noticed that one of the women helping the nuns went to the crib and tried to feed him, but he wouldn't eat.

As a few of us were contemplating what to do, a consecrated woman named Jana made a decision: She was going to spiritually adopt the boy and do everything she could to bring him around, even if he resisted. We were all convinced that what he needed above all was some tender loving care.

Jana picked him up despite the boy's efforts to pull away. He must have been about three years old, but he was somewhat small for lack of proper nutrition. Jana read his tag and saw that his name was Etienne Charles. She sat down with Etienne and tried to calm him down as best she could. The rest of us got back to work among the other children.

After a while Etienne sort of resigned himself to being held. He sat on Jana's lap with a disgruntled look on his face. I passed by Jana a bit later and had a closer look at Etienne. I noticed that his eyes were very blank and empty. He never focused his eyes on anyone; he looked away with a very lost look. As I looked closer his eyes seemed strangely dark. The scowl on his face was not normal for a baby of his age. I also noticed that the skin on his legs was peeling due to his dehydration and malnourishment. Etienne had been scratching his legs quite a bit and his skin was very tender. Behind his right knee he had scratched so much that the skin was an open wound. No doubt it was very painful.

Etienne was in bad shape, but his eyes made me think he was suffering not just in his body but in his spirit.

About an hour later Jana was still holding the boy when she started to pray for Etienne. She herself had noticed his empty eyes and how he would always look away. So she held him close and looked straight into his eyes. As she started praying and asking our Lord for his help for Etienne, the boy in her arms started to fuss and squirm. He had calmed down quite a bit, but as she prayed he became visibly upset. She prayed more and he pulled away even more. When she would stop praying, he would calm down. Jana realized something was up and immediately brought him to me.

I was holding another boy named James when Jana approached. She said: "Father, I think Etienne needs a blessing. Just look what happens when you make the sign of the cross on his forehead."

I curiously traced the sign of the cross with my thumb on his forehead and was met by a reaction I didn't expect. He immediately pulled his head away, moaning and squirming as though I had hurt him.

It then dawned on me what was going on.

Unfortunately many of the children born in the poor tent cities are unwanted, the result of out-of-wedlock pregnancies. In some cases a woman may resort to voodoo to end the child's life or the pregnancy. Other children who are sick are brought to a voodoo medicine man. Whatever had happened to Etienne, it wasn't pleasant. I believe it was some form of demonic oppression rather than possession. He was a child in darkness, and Jana and I were determined to bring him back into the light.

I had been a priest for six months almost to the day when this occurred. I tried to think back to my seminary studies about cases similar to this, but nothing really came to mind. I had taken a brief course on exorcism but not much more. I did know that I couldn't do an exorcism myself, as that is a long process that involves the bishop. Lost in a tent city in Port-au-Prince, I wasn't about to go wandering around looking for the local bishop. But I could give blessings and offer prayers of liberation—sort of the next best thing.

Not really sure what to do and relying on the Holy Spirit and my pastoral instinct, I decided to perform a blessing over Etienne with some holy water and pray for his deliverance from darkness.

I had Jana place him in a nearby crib as I deposited James in another. I looked around for water and found a baby cup on the counter full of water. The baby cup was not really dignified enough for the liturgical use I was going to put it to, but I thought, "Oh well, in missionary work, you use what you have…."

So I blessed the water in the cup and approached Etienne's crib. I placed a stole over my shoulders and then began. Jana was alongside me, praying. Etienne was on his back looking up with a slight scowl on his face. His eyes were empty and dark, and he was staring at the ceiling above us. His arms were held across his chest in a "don't touch me" posture.

I dipped my hand in the holy water and traced a cross on his forehead, his hands, and his chest. I then held both my hands over him and prayed silently for a moment. The words I used for the prayer were simple: "Lord, bring this child out of darkness and into the light. In the name of the Father and of the Son and of the Holy Spirit. Amen."

As soon as I finished making the sign of the cross over Etienne, the most beautiful thing happened. Laying on his back and looking up, Etienne blinked his eyes a few times and shook his head. It was like he suddenly woke up. I saw a spark of life come back into his eyes. The darkness left, and his eyes became alive. He immediately locked his gaze right on Jana, his "adopted" mother. Still holding my hand in blessing over his crib, I mumbled words to the effect of, "Wow, something just happened…"

After a moment of looking at Jana, Etienne unfolded his arms from across his chest and for the first time held up both little arms towards Jana. His expression changed to "Please, please pick me up!"

Jana immediately scooped Etienne out of the crib and held him in a long embrace. Etienne wrapped his arms around her, placed his head on her chest and had a look of wonder and contentment about him, as if he had just come home. As I stood speechless by Jana at what had just happened, Etienne reached out an arm toward me. I was still holding the baby cup full of holy water, and Etienne wanted a drink.

I wasn't sure if holy water was proper for him to drink, but after what had just happened I thought to myself that it couldn't hurt at all. I held it to Etienne's lips as he drank down the whole cup. The holy water was now inside his little body, and I prayed it would keep doing its work!

I have replayed in my mind many times what happened that day. Etienne's eyes are what stick with me the most, with the spark of life jumping back into them. Not that I was skeptical about what happened, I was just not ready to *really* see a change come over Etienne. I guess I lacked a simple, childlike faith!

Etienne then pointed to a bowl of food on the counter. Jana reached for it and sat down with Etienne, and he started eating. Jana fed him spoon after spoon of rice and beans. He finished it and wanted more, so Jana got him another bowl.

Once finished with the second bowl, Etienne settled into Jana's arms. He started laughing and smiling like a normal little boy. He seemed a bit shy still, not really understanding what was happening around him. He was our little miracle child.

The story doesn't end there. The next day when we arrived at the orphanage, Jana, now feeling that Etienne was truly her adopted child, went straight to his crib and picked him up again. That's when we noticed that the back of his knee had healed! The skin that had been raw had now skinned over. Etienne was no longer scratching and suffering from it. We all gave many thanks to God for the event, and I keep his photo on my desktop so as not to forget. Anytime

I need a reminder of God's love for me or a boost in my priesthood, I only have to look at that picture of smiling Etienne!

Now every time I walk through the clinics and orphanages of Haiti and Mexico, I always stop at each bedside and offer blessings and a smile. I know that if Christ were there, that is exactly what he would do.

Sometimes the apostles did not like to see the Master burdened by long lines of mothers and infants, and occasionally they tried to chase them away. However, Christ would have nothing to do with that. We read:

> *The disciples spoke sternly to those who brought them; but Jesus said, "Let the little children come to me, and do not stop them; for it is to such as these that the kingdom of heaven belongs." And he laid his hands on them and went on his way. (Matthew 19:13–15)*

I see so much joy among the people who dedicate time to working in orphanages. I understand now why Christ loved spending time with little children. Their simplicity and faith is refreshing. I am sure it was wearisome and taxing for Christ during the long days he spent among men. So many worldly minded men tried to trap him and argue with him or outdo him in some difficult question. Others wanted favors from him; few thanked him. At the end of a long day among these Pharisee types, it is no wonder Christ loved spending time in Bethany, going off alone to pray to his Father. Even after a long day, when the disciples thought that to help him rest they should turn away the mothers and children, Jesus insisted that they come to him. These moments refreshed him and lifted his spirit. In a similar way, after a long day of working in the orphanage, the missionaries always come home exhausted but happier than they have ever been in their lives. All because the children drew forth from them the one thing necessary in life: love.

Christ loves the simple, truthful soul. Pride and vanity darken the soul and cause it to lose its childlikeness. To approach Christ one need not be wise, well-off, perfect, or highly esteemed. Christ is not demanding of you perfection and impeccability—he simply asks that you strive to love purely with your whole heart. Christ is not like the rulers of the world today. Our Lord desires that we come to him as little children. We can leave behind all our worldly status, diplomas, titles, any trappings of honor. Even our sins and weaknesses can be left behind. Letting go of all these things frees us in a beautiful way. When we become like children, we will experience the freedom of the sons and daughters of God. Above all we will feel the protection and love of our Heavenly Father.

CHAPTER ELEVEN

Christ and Mothers—The Daughter of Jairus

The death of a loved one always causes us pain and confusion, and it can sometimes cause us to question God. *Why death? Why take this person now?* The death of a child only increases this pain and confusion. *Why a life so short-lived? Why bring someone into the world only to take them away so soon?*

When one looks upon death in the light of Christ, however, everything takes on a new color.

We have already reflected upon the scene of Jesus in Magdala regarding the woman with the hemorrhage. Let's revisit it and delve deeper into the events of that day. The story continued with the raising of the little girl from the dead. Christ was on his way to the home of Jairus, where a grief-stricken family was weeping. A group of lamenters had already formed outside the home. The people had reason to be sad: The young girl who just weeks before had been so full of life now lay dead in her bed. Until Christ arrived on the scene, all was dark and gloomy. The people had given up hope. We read:

> *While he was still speaking, some people came from the leader's house to say, "Your daughter is dead. Why trouble the teacher any further?" But overhearing what they said, Jesus said to the leader of the synagogue, "Do not fear, only believe." (Mark 5:35–36)*

"Only believe." As Christ drew nearer to the house of Jairus, all he asked was a little bit of faith. He knew what he was about to do, and he asked Jairus to trust him. Jesus asks this same faith and trust of us when we face similar situations. I found myself in such a situation once in Haiti, and I was blessed to see faith in action.

I was working with a group of missionaries in the Missionaries of Charity's children's home. At the time they had about fifty very sick children. While feeding, bathing, and dressing one child is a challenge for many parents, the reality of fifty babies all needing the same care and love brings daily trials to the sisters. However, with great sanctity and self-sacrifice, a lot of graces, and many little miracles along the way, this children's home was thriving and doing well.

With me were fifteen missionaries all doing their best to show Christ's love to the children. In the midst of all the work, a mother arrived with a little bundle in her arms. Her little daughter, not more than six months old, wasn't feeling well and had a fever.

The sister in charge of the sick children took the baby in her arms. After a brief examination, a few medicines were administered, an IV was started, and the baby was placed in a crib; one more little angel gracing the children's clinic with her presence.

The mother of the baby monitored the crib for a while and then went outside to speak to some of the other moms in the waiting area. Things settled down into the normal hum of activity in the clinic. It was mealtime, and I was busy with the other missionaries feeding bowls of porridge to the children one by one.

About an hour later I noticed commotion by the crib of the newly arrived baby girl; two of the women who helped as nurses in the clinic had gathered around the crib of the baby girl and were frantically trying to resuscitate the child. I realized quickly what was happening and joined the crib side whispering some prayers for the child and giving her a blessing. In a painfully short span of time it was apparent that there was nothing we could do; the baby had died.

This scene is unfortunately all too common in Haiti. The fathers and mothers have very little food to feed their children, and what they do have is of an extremely poor quality and contains little nutritional value. The children rarely get fresh fruits or vegetables, and meat is a luxury. Months and years of a poor diet causes children to be so malnourished and weak that in far too many cases when the children arrive to the clinic it is already too late—the best medicine in the world could not save them.

This case was similar to so many others I had seen. However, this baby girl had appeared very healthy. Her hair was braided neatly; she wore little earrings and a clean dress. Other than the fever there were no signs of illness. Her death was a mystery.

The other missionaries in the room quickly noticed the group of us standing helplessly around the crib. They gathered around and joined me in prayer. Together we prepared ourselves to comfort the mother who had yet to make an appearance.

Soon she came bustling back into the room. She had been outside sitting with the women and a few of the missionaries. She was teaching them to braid their hair the Haitian way. No doubt she had braided the hair of her little daughter earlier that morning before she left home for the clinic.

It was painful to see her look of shock when she saw us gathered around her crib. She ran to the crib and shouted, "No!" as the tears sprang forth. She hovered over the crib, held her baby, and cried and screamed. The commotion around this one child's crib quickly caused the other sick babies to join in the crying. The children's home was in an uproar.

The mother's initial shock wore off and turned into uncontrollable weeping as the awareness of what had just happened sunk in. Her loud sobs and wailing filled the orphanage and the entire compound. All the children were crying, and everyone else became very somber. After about ten minutes by her daughter's crib, the mother went outside and sat in a corner to continue to weep. One of the women present whispered to me that this was the third child she had lost to illness. The woman was yelling at God: "Why do you give me children?"

I had been a priest not even a year, and this was the first time I had to console a grieving family member. I didn't know exactly what to do, but as a priest I knew I had to do something. However, the language barrier prevented me from really speaking to the woman. I approached her and sat next to her for a few moments. I touched her arm to make her aware of my presence, and she briefly glanced at me between loud sobs. I placed my hands upon her head and prayed to Our Lord for strength and healing. She calmed down briefly while I finished the blessing but then immediately began to shake and cry as loudly as before.

A few of the young women missionaries also tried to console her. They hugged her and sang songs, trying anything to ease her pain. Nothing worked. The situation was not really understandable; it seemed so painful, so unnecessary. How could a good God allow this to happen? I knew in my heart there was an answer, but in moments like this, answers are difficult to find; pain and hurt and confusion reign.

After almost an hour, the answer came in the form of a little Missionary of Charity dressed in a white sari with blue trim. This sister was in charge of the clinic and had been away in the chapel at community prayers. We quickly filled her in on what had happened.

She went to the baby's body and confirmed the child's death, then looked out at the mother wailing in the corner. With a look of compassion, she walked directly over to the mother. Sitting down beside her, she placed her arm around the mother and began to speak to her.

Then something happened that none of us expected. Not two minutes had passed since the sister had started speaking, when the woman's crying stopped.

Slowly she stood up, wiped her eyes and dusted herself off. She gathered her purse, walked back into the orphanage and placed a loving hand upon her daughter. After a brief moment she walked out the door and left the clinic to inform her family of what had happened.

We watched the mother's departure in surprise and wondered at how quickly she had pulled herself together. Then all eyes turned to the little sister who had come back into the children's home and was already busying herself with the many tasks at hand. A handful of the missionaries approached her and asked, "Sister, what did you tell her?"

The sister's answer was unforgettable. Just imagine Mother Teresa with a look of faith and confidence added to a voice that spoke with an echo of eternity. She said: "It is very simple. I told her Christ had come to the orphanage today and was blessing all the children. Christ decided he wanted to take your baby home to heaven with him. You had your baby in your arms, and you gave your baby to Jesus. There is nothing to cry about!"

This answer was as simple as it was true. Spoken by the holy Missionary of Charity who had given her life to serve God, the words rang out doubly true. What is death? Death is the encounter of the soul with Christ. Death certainly is unnatural for us since we, as humans, are created to exist with both body and soul. Any separation of the two is an unnatural state and naturally feared. However, when supernaturally understood, death is the definitive encounter with Christ. This baby was undoubtedly in the arms of Christ, and there she would remain for all eternity. The mother would be reunited in the future with this child. The passing of this child into eternity was a moment for sorrow but not despair.

The simple words of the nun put everything into perspective for the woman. And while she still exhibited deep sorrow, she was no longer falling into despair. She pulled herself together, and faith allowed her to carry on with life.

We all learned a lesson that day in the children's home. As the years go by and I witness more sick and dying children, the truth that they will be forever in the arms of Christ is clear.

Through the light of Christ, we can truly say with St. Paul:

> *Death has been swallowed up in victory.*
> *Where, O death, is your victory?*
> *Where, O death, is your sting? (1 Corinthians 15:54–55)*

After seeing how the hands of Christ reach out to us and how he daily walks along the road of life with us, let us return to the Gospel passage. We left Christ on his way to the home of Jairus. Before Jesus arrived, the home is symbolic of afflicted souls in need of grace. In their problems and crisis moments, without an eternal vision provided by the person of Christ, everything seemed impossible, and they fell into despair. When Christ entered into the home, however, all was made right.

I can't imagine the empty pain and despair that lack of knowledge of Christ can bring. A life lived with Christ doesn't mean there are never any difficulties. This is not the case. In fact those who grow closer to Christ will receive a great gift: that of the cross and the opportunity to participate in the redemptive work of Christ. They have the grace to become more like our Lord by offering their own sufferings to the Father with Christ.

When Christ arrived at the home of Jairus, all was made right.

> *When they came to the house of the leader of the synagogue, he saw a commotion, people weeping and wailing loudly. When he had entered, he said to them, "Why do you make a commotion and weep? The child is not dead but sleeping." And they laughed at him. Then he put them all outside, and took the child's father and mother and those who were with him, and went in where the child was. He took her by the hand and*

said to her, "Talitha cum," which means, "Little girl, get up!" And immediately the girl got up and began to walk about (she was twelve years of age). At this they were overcome with amazement. (Mark 5:38–42)

Christ became the Lord of Jairus's home. Now Jairus could say with Joshua in the Old Testament: "For me and my household: We will serve the Lord! (Joshua 24:15).

To know Christ is to know Truth itself. To know Christ is to know Love itself. A life lived with Christ, no matter how difficult, always has purpose and meaning; sacrifice is redemptive; love always wins. *When Christ enters your life, all of your problems become beautiful crosses that you begin to carry alongside Christ.* A cross may be difficult, but crosses are always positive and redemptive because they lead you to the glory of the Resurrection. There you will stand alongside Christ in his glory. The size of your cross on earth will be the size of your crown in heaven!

CHAPTER TWELVE

Christb and Fathers

A father is called to be the spiritual leader of the home. He provides for and protects his family. He has an important role in preparing his children for life in the world. The call to fatherhood is a call to be very Christlike. Christ comes into our lives as a protection from sin and death, providing grace for our souls and preparing us for eternal life. This is why he understands so well the role of a father and why it is no wonder that fathers have a special place in the merciful heart of Christ.

Christ's great love for fathers comes from his experience with his foster father, St. Joseph. He spent many years in the carpentry shop helping Joseph with the daily tasks. The Gospels tell us that the Child Jesus grew in wisdom; much of this wisdom came from the quiet virtue he saw in St. Joseph. Years of work alongside Joseph formed and molded the young Jesus. His foster father was a man of prayer—he made work a prayer; he made life a gift. Joseph was a man of quiet strength and few words. It was this silence that spoke volumes to the Christ Child.

In the love of Joseph for Jesus, Our Lord saw manifested in a human way the divine love of God the Father for his children on earth. St. John Paul II rightly refers to the depths of this father-son relationship in Nazareth as a "mystery."

We know that Jesus addressed God with the word "Abba"—a loving,

familiar word that would have been used by children in first-century
Palestine when speaking to their fathers. Most probably Jesus, like other
children, used this same word when speaking to St. Joseph. Can any more
be said about the mystery of human fatherhood? Jesus himself, as a man,
experienced the fatherhood of God through that father-son relationship
with Saint Joseph. This filial encounter with Joseph then fed into Our
Lord's revelation of the paternal name of God. What a profound mystery![1]

At Sunday Mass, as I look out at the congregation, I see many families sitting together. Parents sit proudly on either side of the pew with their children in between. Many are dressed in their Sunday best. During Communion these families come up together, the father bringing up the rear. Each one takes his or her turn, and I place the sacred host in their outstretched hands or on their tongues. Many different types of hands reach out: small hands, large hands, manicured hands, dirty hands. Yet the ones that always catch my attention are the calloused hands of the father; they are a testament to hard work done out of love for their children. These hands, which become arthritic and painful with time, are very precious in the eyes of God.

How many times did Jesus see the hands of St. Joseph, calloused and worn from his carpentry work, reach out to embrace him? Eventually Christ would stretch out his own hands upon the cross and receive the nails, embracing the whole world.

One day all of us will stand before Our Lord and he will ask us to stretch out our hands. A father's daily struggle to work and provide for his family may not seem great in the grand scheme of things, but in the eyes of Christ, there are few more beautiful lives than those that resemble the life of his beloved foster father, Joseph. Their hands may not hold great works of evangelization, hospitals

---

1   John Paul II, *Rise, Let Us Be On Our Way!* (New York: Warner Books, 2004), 139.

and schools, and years of missionary work. But these hands themselves are a testament to great love! In eternity as these men stretch out their hands before our Lord, not a word needs to be spoken. God the Father sees in these men the image of his Son. He welcomes them into heaven.

We have reflected upon one father already, revealed to us in the story of Jairus's daughter. Jairus was a good father who was unafraid to bring Christ into his home. Let us reflect on another father in the Gospel, one who was unafraid to go out and bring his broken family to Christ. Our story begins with Christ at his transfiguration.

Six days later, Jesus took with him Peter and James and John, and led them up a high mountain apart, by themselves. And he was transfigured before them, and his clothes became dazzling white, such as no one on earth could bleach them. And there appeared to them Elijah with Moses, who were talking with Jesus. (Mark 9:2–4)

Jesus ascended the mountain, allowing his physical actions to reflect a deeper spiritual reality: he was going to pray to his Father and so spiritually ascended the heights of his Father's will. Jesus ascended both the physical mountain and the spiritual mountain of prayer, taking with him his closest apostles because he wanted to share the presence of God the Father with them. So often Jesus would go off alone to pray and be alone with his Father, but he desired to reveal to the apostles the greatest truth of their lives: the fatherly love of God. His physical transformation provoked awe in the three chosen apostles, but so did the close relationship Christ had with his Father. "Then a cloud overshadowed them, and from the cloud there came a voice, 'This is my Son, the Beloved; listen to him!'" (Mark 9:7).

The apostles heard the voice of the Father and were penetrated by the love that surrounded Jesus. In this moment Christ, high up and away from the cares of the world, was bathed in light and love, the object of his Father's divine love.

The descent down the mountain is just as important. While at the top Christ's Fatherhood was revealed in its perfection, at the bottom an earthly example of fatherhood awaited the apostles for them to contemplate—and for us to contemplate, too. The ascent and descent are not separate events joined together in the Gospel by chance. The divine Father-Son relationship is the ideal; it is the source of all father-son bonds, and it is only in Jesus's relationship with his Father that we learn the fullness and beauty of earthly fatherhood.

As they were coming down the mountain, he ordered them to tell no one about what they had seen, until after the Son of Man had risen from the dead. When they came to the disciples, they saw a great crowd around them, and some scribes arguing with them. When the whole crowd saw him, they were immediately overcome with awe, and they ran forward to greet him. (Mark 9:9, 14–15)

A crowd gathered around Our Lord, and in the front was a father with his son.

He asked them, "What are you arguing about with them?" Someone from the crowd answered him, "Teacher, I brought you my son; he has a spirit that makes him unable to speak; and whenever it seizes him, it dashes him down; and he foams and grinds his teeth and becomes rigid; and I asked your disciples to cast it out, but they could not do so." (Mark 9:16–18)

While Christ was on top of the mountain with his Father, the rest of the apostles—the nine who stayed behind—were busy trying to expel a demon.

Three chapters earlier in the Gospel of Mark, the apostles had been given authority over demons. They spent considerable time going two by two to all the villages, continuing the saving work of Christ. The Gospels are silent about actual events among the apostles during these journeys, but surely the fame of Christ and his band of twelve apostles was widespread. The attention usually focused on Christ as the source of their power, but without Christ himself it is probable that the apostles themselves were held in wonder and esteem by the crowds.

This day, however, their spiritual authority seems compromised. Nothing seems to work. Where Jesus is absent, there is no peace and light: Darkness reigns. Much like the mother in Haiti in the previous chapter, without Christ there is despair. With Christ there is hope. So when Christ arrived on the scene, the nine apostles gratefully stepped back and allowed him to take center stage.

Jesus addressed the father; his heart went out to the man's plight. The boy was brought before him, and the demon, sensing the presence of Christ, became furious and desperate and threw the boy's body into convulsions. In an uncharacteristic move Our Lord paused to get some more background on the child before he expelled the demon. Our Lord knows everything; yet he likes to hear our prayers and needs spoken in faith. He allowed the father to make his prayer:

Jesus asked the father, "How long has this been happening to him?" And he said, "From childhood. It has often cast him into the fire and into the water, to destroy him; but if you are able to do anything, have pity on us and help us." (Mark 9:21–22)

The story became clearer. The son was not a small boy anymore, since the father referenced his son's past childhood. We can assume the boy was in his teens. For years then, the demon has thrown him into fire and water. We might ask ourselves: "Who always dove into the water to save the boy? Who was burned over and over again while pulling the boy out of the fire?" These questions reveal something beautiful about the type of man the father is. He has spent his life caring for and protecting this child. Every time the boy needed help his father was there.

The Gospel reveals a secret about fatherhood here: A true father centers his life on his family. A family-centered life is the calling of every father. When a father knows this, there is peace in the family. When the father has a self-centered approach to life, focusing more on his hobbies and whims, family problems begin.

Notice also how the father referred to his son's situation as something that affected both of them. He asked for pity on "us"; he asked Christ to help "us." The father saw his son as part of his life. If the son was doing poorly, so was the father. If the son was healed, they were both healed.

Christ witnessed this great love of the father for his son and thought of his own heavenly Father. The Father in heaven is the perfect father, and whatever happened to Christ the Son happened to the Father. Christ knew that, just as this earthly father jumped into fire to save his son, so his Heavenly father would be present with him at the cross; he would pull the Son from the fires of death and raise him up in glory in heaven.

In the midst of suffering—especially the suffering of a beloved child—a parent might ask, "Doesn't God care? Where is the Father in this difficult situation? Why doesn't he intervene?" God the Father knows how we feel. He, too, witnessed the suffering of his Son. His hope for us is to say with this father in our Gospel story, "Lord, I believe, help my unbelief!"

One day in Haiti, while I was with a group of missionaries in the children's home, a man brought in his infant son. The father explained that the child's mother had died in childbirth, leaving him to care for his son alone. Due to extreme poverty he was making great sacrifices to keep his son fed and cared for. When he realized that the son had an illness that was beyond his ability to care for, he made the long journey to the clinic.

The father watched as his son was admitted into the clinic and given an IV. He saw which crib his son was placed in, and then he held his son for about an hour before he had to leave. He lived and worked on the other side of Port-au-Prince, and the trip on foot was a very long one. He left his son in the care of the holy sisters. This happened on a Monday morning.

The father did not come back all week. He was too poor to visit his son, and he had no phone or any means to communicate with the clinic. As the days went by, the sisters and the missionary students I had with me took care of the boy. We held him, knowing that human touch was a key element in his healing process.

By Friday morning the boy was doing much better and no longer needed an IV. That morning the father made his reappearance. He entered the door of the clinic with a worried and anxious look. He headed straight for the back corner where he had left his son five days earlier. The look of worry on his face told the tale: Since the moment he left on Monday he was not sure if his son was still alive. He had no way to find out until he was once again able to make the long journey on foot to the clinic. All week he had prayed and hoped that his son was recovering. Only when he saw his son that Friday morning did his worry change to overwhelming joy.

The man picked up his son and embraced him lovingly and began to thank the sisters for their help. I will never forget the joy on the father's face as he was reunited with his son, and I can only think that the face of the father who brought his possessed son to Jesus and received him back as a new creation must have had that same expression of joy.

When Jesus saw that a crowd came running together, he rebuked the unclean spirit, saying to it, "You spirit that keeps this boy from speaking and hearing, I command you, come out of him, and never enter him again!" After crying out and convulsing him terribly, it came out, and the boy was like a corpse, so that most of them said, "He is dead." But Jesus took him by the hand and lifted him up, and he was able to stand. (Mark 9:25–27)

The father and son were reunited, and with his mind now restored, the young man was finally able to see the loving face of his father and his many scars of love.

Every father has his own scars of love, whether they are seen or not. Some bear the visible scars of exhaustion and fatigue from a hard day's labor, while others carry the interior struggle of not being able to provide all that they would like for their children. Still others carry the wound of estrangement or the struggle of watching their children walk down a road they do not approve of. Our Father in heaven bore the first wound of love when Adam and Eve turned away from him, and Jesus himself bears forever in heaven his scars of love, the price of our redemption.

Therefore, if you are a father, show your love for your wife and children through your every action. Never be ashamed of your work-worn hands when you go up to Communion. I believe Our Lord is delighted to be received by someone whose very life and body has become a symbol of generous love. It reminds him of the calloused hands of St. Joseph which so many times held him as a child.

On a final note: Fathers, pray for your children! When all is said and done and your children grow up and leave home to begin their own lives, what God wishes for you to do at that point is to pray. Children should always be enveloped in the prayer of their parents. And pray without growing weary, for as Our Lord said to St. Gertrude the Great:

> Do not... be surprised if you do not see the fruits of your prayers with your bodily eyes, since I dispose of them, according to My eternal Wisdom, to greater advantage. And know that the more you pray for anyone, the happier they will become, because no prayer of faith can remain unfruitful, although we do not know in what manner it will fructify.[2]

Even if it seems all is lost, Our Lord wishes for us to keep praying, for anyone who brings his or her family to Christ, like the father in this Gospel story, will not walk away disappointed.

---

2 St. Gertrude the Great, *The Writings and Revelations of St. Gertrude* (Rockford, Ill.: TAN Books and Publications, 2002), 192.

PART THREE

CHRIST IN YOUR LIFE

CHAPTER THIRTEEN

Christ and the Missionary Mandate

The Gospels end their narratives of the earthly life of Christ with his ascension.

> *Then he led them out as far as Bethany, and, lifting up his hands, he blessed them. While he was blessing them, he withdrew from them and was carried up into heaven. And they worshiped him, and returned to Jerusalem with great joy; and they were continually in the temple blessing God. (Luke 24:50–53)*

Christ ascended to the Father on a cloud, much to the amazement of his disciples. He blessed them, breathing on them the Holy Spirit. Above all he gave them a command: to go to all nations and make disciples. Every Christian is called to be an apostle, and every Christian community a living flame of the Church.

This summon to go to all nations has been taken very seriously by the Church down through the centuries. It is her essential mission: the salvation of mankind in Christ through establishing his kingdom on earth. This mission consists in bringing the greatest number of people to know God's love deeply, living in love by practicing the authentic and generous charity Christ preached and demanded, and striving to make God's merciful love known

I SAW HIS FACE

to all mankind by tirelessly preaching the Gospel. The power of Christ's love cannot be contained! With St. Paul the Church says: "Woe to me if I do not proclaim the gospel!" (1 Corinthians 9:16).

The Church is always in "mission mode," bringing Christ's message throughout history to all corners of the earth. The glorious chronicles of the Church tell the tale of holy missionaries, both men and women, who gave their lives for the Gospel in foreign lands. They are part of the most glorious history of the Church. But the chronicles of the Church are not a thing of the past. Even today every Catholic is called to be a missionary in some way.

Because of this worldwide missionary spirit, our Catholic faith has spread to all corners of the globe and truly has become what its name in Greek signifies: *universal.* In every continent, in every country, in every land you may travel, you will surely find faithful Catholics. Whether it's a small, persecuted remnant in China or Saudi Arabia, lost in the mountains and hills of Latin America, or walking the streets of New York City, you will find that Christ is very much alive.

One Holy Week I led a mission trip in Haiti for about twenty college students from the Midwest. It was Good Friday, and we were on our way to help Fr. Wagner, the parish priest of a village located about thirty miles outside of Port-au-Prince. His new church needed repairs, and his many villagers were eager for special activities during Holy Week.

We decided the night before that we would help him with the living Way of the Cross. A number of the missionaries would act out parts of the stations—not a difficult thing to organize. However, as we were bouncing down the dirt roads in our vehicle toward the village that morning, I began to have some doubts. None of the kids with me spoke Creole. None of them had ever been to Haiti before, so they were unfamiliar with the culture. None of us had any idea what the Way of the Cross would look like or what exactly we were supposed to do. We were just hoping it would all work out!

The village was located in a very green and forested part of Haiti, at the base of a few large hills. As we pulled up to the village, I noticed a dirt road where all the villagers had gathered already at the first station. We jumped out of the truck, and I began organizing the missionaries. I assigned the different roles—one would be Mary, another Veronica, another Simon, etc.

We quickly caught up with the villagers, and I held my breath as I waited to find out just exactly we had gotten ourselves into.

We approached the procession and heard the Haitians singing in Creole a hymn we all recognized. We couldn't sing the words, but we could hum along. The stations were set up outside the homes of the different village families. The path of the stations formed a wide circuit around the village. As we stopped before each station, the family stepped out of their home and greeted us. Each station was made out of branches and sheets and decorated with flowers and colorful rocks.

When we arrived at the fourth station, Jesus Meets His Mother, the young woman I had selected to be Mary knelt before the Haitian man representing Jesus. She wept softly as one of the faithful read from the Gospel. Fr. Wagner began by saying in Creole: "We adore you, O Christ, and we praise you!" Then, genuflecting, we all responded: "Because by your holy cross you have redeemed the world!" Someone stood up and read a passage from the Holy Father. Next Fr. Wagner led everyone in a prayer. We then thanked the family and proceeded to the next station about a quarter mile down the road. As we walked, we sang and hummed the Church's hymns.

As I walked alongside Fr. Wagner at the back of the procession, I was impressed by the universality of the Church. Here we were, a bunch of strangers in a strange land, yet even here in the jungle, we found our brothers and sisters in the faith. We were able to join right in with them in praising God. No questions asked; no answers needed. We were one family, and we knew just what to do. The Way of the Cross is the same in the jungle village of Haiti as it is in the basilicas in Rome and the parishes in America. Our Church truly is universal.

Some missionaries arrived in Haiti many years ago, bringing the good news. Those same missionaries had been evangelized by another missionary, who was evangelized by another missionary, and so on all the way back to the Upper Room with the first apostles. It was because those apostles obeyed Christ's message and went out into the world to make disciples that you and I received the faith.

This doesn't mean we can sit back and enjoy life now. We must look to the future, to all the many souls out in the world who don't know Christ. There is always a sense of urgency to the mission of the Church. Unfortunately at times this urgency has been lost due to an overly institutional approach. In lands where the original missionary work is over and a diocese and parishes have been established, the faithful sometimes loses touch with the missionary nature of the Church. We get lost in committee meetings, in budget planning, and bingo games. A quote from then Cardinal Ratzinger comes to mind:

> *Wherever a diocesan forum convenes or anything else of the kind takes place, you already know what questions are going to be posed: celibacy, women's ordination, and the remarriage of divorced persons. Those are definitely serious problems.... But in the midst of all this, there is too little attention to the fact that 80 percent of the people of this world are non-Christians who are waiting for the gospel.... We shouldn't be constantly agonizing over our own questions but should be pondering how we as Christians can express today in this world what we believe and thereby say something to those people. In the consciousness of the Church, ...a massive narrowing has taken place. We look only at ourselves; we are concerned only with ourselves; we lick our wounds; we want to construct*

a nice Church for ourselves and hardly see any longer that the Church doesn't exist for herself but that we have a word that has something to say to the world and ought to be heard.[1]

One of my favorite things to do when I studied in Rome was to go to St. Peter's Basilica for early morning Mass. The basilica has many side altars where priests may celebrate Mass. On the ground floor there are only a few altars, but down below in the crypt that surrounds the burial place of Peter, there are many more altars and chapels. It was here that I loved to go.

The large doors of the basilica open promptly at 7:00 a.m. The doors swing open in the early pre-dawn light, and the basilica is hushed and quiet. Light filters in through Michelangelo's windows, shining down in shafts that pierce the large nave and give it a heavenly glow. In the center of the church under the dome is a set of spiral stairs that leads to the crypt below. It is almost a secret passageway that descends right under the basilica.

Here many small chapels have been built around the main altar. In this catacomb-like structure, everywhere one turns one is greeted with a beautiful sight: dozens of chapels all in use, with different languages and different songs blending together as the voice of the Church in prayer. At the same time there are Africans and Americans, French and Japanese, Mexicans and Lebanese, all praising God through the sacrifice of the Mass. Hearing the different languages and ways of singing and seeing the different peoples and colors and clothing, one understands a deep reality: The Catholic Church is universal; it embraces all nations and cultures.

All are welcome. One need not be part of the African group to jump right into their service, nor does one need to know their language. The rubrics and flow of the Mass are universal. I may not be able to say the exact words, but I

---

1 Josef Cardinal Ratzinger, *Salt of the Earth* (San Francisco: Ignatius Press, 1997), 160.

know exactly what is going on. This universality unites the Church across continents and cultures.

Once I invited two Protestant friends to St. Peter's Basilica for early morning Mass. They were shocked at the enormous number of people present, as well as the variety of languages and songs. But above all, what surprised them was the way we simply looked for any random Mass about to begin and joined a complete group of strangers to worship together. What for me was the most natural thing, for them was unheard of. You didn't, at least in their branch of Protestantism, ever just walk into another church uninvited! Mother Church, as the arms of the colonnade in St. Peter's plaza represent, has her motherly arms open to embrace the whole world.

Who are these arms today? It is nice to speak figuratively of the arms of Mother Church, but in reality the Church is alive in each one of us. We aren't a Church of places and times—we are a Church of the sacraments, and where her faithful are gathered to celebrate these sacraments, there Mother Church is present.

Once Christ ascended into heaven, the missionary phase of the Church Militant began. We are all called to participate in this work. As we have seen throughout this book, Christ comes to transform us. Our lives change upon meeting Christ. We cannot remain the same. It is impossible to envision a Christ without a message or a command or a plan for your life. That is not who Christ is.

It is an error to reduce the encounter with Christ to an emotional feeling. Many contemporary youth retreats include music or activities that bring out a deep feeling of peace. However, so many times this warm fuzzy feeling does not go deep into the soul to transform it. Saul became the Apostle Paul after he encountered Christ, a meeting that went painfully deep for Saul but one that convinced him of the need to radically change his life forever.

It is an error to reduce Christ to a Sunday obligation, as if the focus of all Christ's work was to get all humanity to an hour-long service each Sunday.

It is an error to reduce Christ to a warm, fuzzy, welcoming, passive person. This Jesus is not the real Jesus. Jesus accepts sinners in order to to transform them, not confirm them in their sin.

The encounter with Christ, just as it was for every person in the Gospel, is transformative. Each and every person with whom Jesus deals is changed; no one can stay the same.

For two thousand years the Mystical Body of Christ has preached Christ and worked out of love for Christ in response to this encounter.

On a missionary trip to Mexico, I had a singular experience. I was in charge of leading a busload of high school boys to the mountains of Veracruz. We were on our way to build two homes and re-roof many houses in the mountains around Orizaba. I also was planning to go house-to-house, visiting the sick and inviting the villagers to the Church for the sacraments.

Due to the mountainous dirt roads, it took us a very long time to get to the village. We finally arrived after sundown, about 8:00 p.m. in the evening. The villagers had been expecting us, so an official delegation greeted us at the local church. It was by then a sleepy village. About thirty huts were clustered around the church, and roosters, chickens, sheep, and donkeys were wandering around just about everywhere. The village was situated high up on the mountain, and we could see some small lights from other huts far in the distance. The bus pulled up by the church, and I stepped off to speak with the village leaders.

When the village leaders saw my Roman collar, one asked if I was a priest. I said yes. His eyes lit up and he quickly asked: "Would you say Mass for us tomorrow?"

It was Saturday night, and the villagers were not expecting to have a priest to say the Sunday Mass. I replied, "Of course! I will say Mass for you every day I am here."

He was visibly moved and then scampered off towards the church. I watched him enter the church and then climb the bell tower. When he reached the top, he grabbed hold of the rope and started ringing the church bell loudly. The tolls of the bell echoed back from across the mountain and could no doubt be heard from miles around. I watched with interest as he rang the bell a dozen times and then picked up a megaphone.

He said loudly enough to be heard by all the huts around the church: "We have a priest in the village! Tomorrow we will have Mass at eight o'clock. The missionaries have arrived!"

What a beautiful welcome! I translated the message to the missionaries around me who were just getting off the bus. Some words from Scripture came to mind:

> *How beautiful upon the mountains*
> *are the feet of the messenger who announces peace,*
> *who brings good news,*
> *who announces salvation,*
> *who says to Zion, "Your God reigns."*
> *Listen! Your sentinels lift up their voices,*
> *together they sing for joy;*
> *for in plain sight they see*
> *the return of the Lord to Zion. (Isaiah 52:7–8)*

The mission of Christ continues even today. He still affects the lives of millions of people. Anywhere a disciple of Christ preaches, Christ's voice is still heard. Where a missionary walks, Christ walks. Where a disciple cares for the sick or feeds the hungry, Christ is there. Christ desires that you be his hands and feet!

CHAPTER FOURTEEN

Christ the Merciful King

Even at the end of this book, the person of Christ is still a mystery. He is infinite in majesty, and we will never fully fathom his divine depths. He is akin to a story never *fully* told and an icon never fully revealed. Yet a mystery is not something we can't know—it is something we can never fully know. Like a museum of unending rooms filled with artwork that one will never come to the end of exploring, the mystery of Christ is one that the souls in heaven will spend all eternity contemplating. We call this the Beatific Vision, gazing on the face of God.

While we can never know Christ fully, we can come to an *adequate* picture of who Christ is through the Scriptures, Sacred Tradition, and the teaching Magisterium of the Holy Father and our bishops. The true icon of Christ has never been better understood throughout the two-thousand-year history of the Church than it is today. Each new Christian stands on the shoulders of those who came before and peers a little farther and deeper into the Mystery of Christ. Thus, the Church, through her faithful sons and daughters, discovers ever more the richness of Christ.

The gift of Christ is not confined only to theologians and consecrated souls: Christ is for all mankind. Thus it is that in all the faithful of the Church, young and old, united as his Mystical Body, we can see the true face of Christ. His true icon emerges amidst the varied and unique experiences of each and every Christian.

Like a diamond of many facets, the person of Christ can be contemplated from many perspectives. One of these facets that integrates all the elements of Christ into a single idea is the image of Christ the Merciful King. His kingdom is love, and his greatest power is his mercy.

The Church herself has highlighted this perspective of Christ as King in her liturgy. The liturgical calendar of the Church, which starts anew every Advent, culminates in late November every year. As a way of drawing to a close and summing up all of who Christ is, we celebrate the Feast of Christ the King on the last Sunday of the Liturgical year. One feels the liturgy building up little by little as the weeks of Ordinary Time go by.

Christ came to establish his Father's kingdom. In the Gospel of Mark at the very beginning we have the words of Christ: "The time is fulfilled, and the kingdom of God has come near; repent, and believe in the good news" (Mark 1:15).

Christ was bent on doing his Father's will. His mission in life encompassed his entire being. He took on our human nature fully so as to pass through death and arrive at the resurrection. This event was the definitive victory of the kingdom of God over the kingdom of sin and death.

When Christ taught his disciples to pray, he instructed them to pray: "Father, hallowed be your name. Your kingdom come" (Luke 11:2).

The phrase *Thy kingdom come!* expresses both theological hope in the definitive coming of the kingdom of Christ as well as the ardent desire and the urgent need to work now in order to establish that kingdom.

The Church must always promote a powerful and personal experience of the love of Christ and seek to make him reign in the hearts of men and in society.

Every king has a throne. In our worldly view, thrones signify power and dynasty. Castles are built, lands are subdued, dynasties extend.

Christ's kingdom is analogous but infinitely greater. He has a throne, he has a castle; and his kingdom never ends.

Yet his throne is different. On earth he reigned from the cross. He came for one purpose: to do the Father's will. The Father's will was for Christ to show his love for us by dying on the cross. Therefore, on the cross Christ fulfilled his Father's mission. This was also the peak and climax of Christ's love for his Father. There on the cross Christ pronounced his eternal word of love to the Father. It was his greatest moment and highest glory, although in the eyes of the world it was total failure.

All disciples of Christ must imitate their king. They must reign from their own personal crosses. All that happens to the Master must happen to the disciple. Christ pronounced his word of love once from the cross. Once the word was pronounced, afterward he simply repeats it in the soul of each member of his Mystical Body. By embracing the cross, the soul glorifies God and imitates Christ. This is our sanctification: the work of the Holy Spirit painting the image of Christ in us. This work takes time and patience, and ultimately it requires embracing the cross.

Christ has few lovers of his cross but many who love his gifts. Everyone wants to be with Christ in the joyful moments of the miracles and on Mt. Tabor. Few, however, follow the Master on the Royal Road of Calvary. Accepting the cross has no appeal to our human nature, which is wounded by sin, yet it remains a necessary avenue to holiness and apostolic effectiveness. *The Cross is the path Christ himself chose to fulfill his work, and it is the path he chooses for his beloved followers.*

> *Then Jesus said to his disciples, 'If anyone wants to be a follower of mine, let him renounce himself and take up his cross and follow me. Anyone who wants to save his life will lose it; but anyone who loses his life for my sake will find it. (Matthew 16:24)*

God's Plan for the Journey

Carrying the cross can be a daunting task and will lead us down roads we may not wish to take. While on another mission trip in Puebla, Mexico, I had an experience that illustrated this for me. On that particular day I was a little worried as I was bouncing along a dusty road in a Chevy pickup. For a week I had been guiding a group of forty missionaries in the hills of Puebla. Work was being done in two different sites about five miles apart. Slowly two small homes for poor families were being constructed. Daily I went back and forth to each site to oversee the projects, and this day wasn't going as I planned.

I had just checked the gas gauge and discovered that the needle was on the red. I wasn't familiar with the truck and didn't know just how long I could keep going until I ran out of fuel. I was ten miles from the nearest gas station, so I decided that, instead of heading to the next work site, I would let the truck coast into town and pray that I would make it. That was my plan. God had a different one.

My plan included no stops or interruptions. God's plan included a young woman with a baby in her arms. She appeared around a bend in the road. She pleaded with her eyes for me to stop, and obeying a natural instinct to help someone in need, I promptly brought the truck to a halt. It looked like she was going my way, it was a hot dry day, and she wouldn't have to walk all the way to her destination if I could give her a ride.

However, her road wasn't exactly my road. She opened her bundle to reveal a very frail and sickly looking baby girl, about six months old. I had seen so many frail children in Haiti and Mexico that I knew this baby had to get to a doctor immediately. The mother began spilling her story in a breathless account. The baby had diarrhea, wouldn't eat or drink, and had a high fever. One thing was certain: The baby needed an IV right away. I told the young mother I would take her to the town where the gas station was located and we could get help. She promptly said no—she had to get to a village in the opposite direction called Santa Marta. I mentally located Santa Marta on the map; there was no gas station there.

I didn't want to abandon the mother, but neither did I want to be stuck in the middle of nowhere without gas; I had to choose. I think God chose that moment to intervene. I looked down at the gas tank and saw that the needle was now hovering just *above* the red line. Was it a sign? Maybe I *did* have enough gas.

I grudgingly turned the truck around and headed down a different road, confident that God was going to get me where I needed to go. As we drove I tried to flag down other cars, but no one could take the mother and child. As we got to the top of the hill and the worst of the journey was behind us, I thought that perhaps she could walk the rest of the way. However, at the top of the hill was a crew of rough-looking miners working on an oil pipeline. She immediately begged me not to leave her with them, as they couldn't be trusted. I peered out of the truck at them and sure enough, they were a scruffy bunch. I couldn't leave her in that situation, so we kept driving. I kept looking every few seconds at the needle, praying it would stay above the red line.

As we continued on, I prepared for the worst—getting stuck in the middle of nowhere and having to spend the rest of the day walking to find gas with all the missionaries oblivious as to where I had vanished.

At one point the rough ride knocked my water bottle to the floor, and as I picked it up, a brief thought struck me: water and a sick baby, all in one truck. Baptism! I turned to the mother and asked if the baby was baptized. She said no.

I brought the truck to a halt and went around to the passenger side. I opened the door, and there with my water bottle I baptized little baby Heriberta. She was now a daughter of God—eternity had entered into her life!

As I got back into the truck, now thankful that God had this woman cross my path, a truck pulled up and very willingly offered to take the mother into the town. I turned my truck around and headed back down the road. Everything became bright and cheery, and I wasn't worried about the gas anymore. What was walking a whole day for gas when we had just given Heribierta the greatest gift of her life? Even the miners waved to me as I drove by.

I kept coasting as much as possible and to my relief, was able to nurse the truck into the gas station. As I headed back out to the mission site with a full tank of gas, I realized again how God's ways aren't our ways. If I had stuck to my plans, however rational and logical they were, I would have not picked up that woman. If I had had my way, perhaps the work on the houses would have progressed a little faster and I would not have had to travel back and forth as much. But all that would merely be my own human achievements.

When God takes over and is at work, there is always the unmistakable mark of the Divine. Where God is allowed to work in a soul, beautiful things happen, and not merely human things. Heriberta's baptism was the most beautiful event of that whole day. God writes straight with crooked lines. Sometimes it is only after many twists and turns on the path that we come into the light and see clearly. God was writing the story that day, and I am glad I allowed him to do it.

Every king has certain subjects called vassals who willingly or unwillingly serve him in order to gain protection and welfare. The agreement is a social pact and written on paper. Each party gives something and receives something.

Christ the King certainly has subjects, too, but quite a different sort. He is not bound to us by a legal contract written on paper but by love written on our hearts. Our baptism transforms us into his children, not by a mere legal adoption but by a true transformation into his children, a change deeper than our very DNA. We are children of the king. This is why he is a *merciful* king, a king of love. He is not like an earthly king who wields power and authority over subjects. His is a family kingdom; he rules over his children with love.

In a very simple passage in the Diary of St. Faustina, we find a beautiful truth revealed. She writes:

> *In a soul that lives on My love alone, I reign as in heaven. I watch over it day and night. In it I find My happiness; My ear is attentive to each request of its heart; often I anticipate its requests.... But child, you are not yet in your homeland; so go fortified by My grace, and fight for My kingdom in human souls; fight as a king's child would; and remember that the days of your exile will pass quickly, and with them the possibility of earning merit for heaven.*[1]

The key phrase here is a "king's child." Christ asks her to fight as a king's child would. On the one hand he wishes her to serve him and fight for him as a subject does. Christ is the Lord of her mission. This means that her whole being will revolve around the king's will, around extending and maintaining his kingdom. Where the king fights, so does the loyal subject. All Christians are called to apply themselves diligently to the service of the king.

On the other hand there is the beautiful truth that through our baptism we are all children of God. We are princes and princesses in God's kingdom. We don't just serve our king; we *love* our King. Christ is both the *Lord of our mission* and the *Love of our life.* Every day we are to lovingly contemplate him in prayer, filling our hearts with his presence and enjoying him. After our prayer we are to daily serve him in the souls of all we meet—this is our mission in life. Prayer causes our hearts to be filled with his love, which then overflows to all we meet. We are called to be always contemplative and always active.

---

1 *Diary*, 1489.

While subjects on a battlefield can be little more than paid mercenaries, a child of the king is there fighting out of an innermost desire to love and serve his Father. In the dark moments of a battle, mercenaries might drop their weapons and flee, but the children of the king maintain their vigilance and fight alongside the king until the end, no matter how dark.

In the Gospel Christ talks about his kingdom chiefly through parables. In these parables he sheds light on the coming of the kingdom. While Christ the King is now present within the heart of each Christian, the kingdom is awaiting a final moment of fulfillment. This will be Christ the King's triumph at the end of time. His last words to us in Scripture speak of his triumphant return: "See, I am coming soon; my reward is with me, to repay according to everyone's work. I am the Alpha and the Omega, the first and the last, the beginning and the end" (Revelation 22:12–13).

The kingdom is like a mustard seed that starts small but then becomes a large plant. The kingdom is unseen like the yeast in the dough, but because it is there the dough rises and expands. The kingdom will be like a king who settles accounts with his subjects.

The message is clear, Christ is King now, but in the end his kingship will be made visible everywhere—not a shred of darkness will remain. No one will question his Lordship; all will bend the knee at the name of Jesus. How beautiful that will be, when all of us will surround the throne of our King in heaven. Each of his true sons and daughters will join hands as they joyfully bend their knees to pay him homage. Then all of creation will sing the praises of God:

> *Holy, Holy, Holy, the Lord God the Almighty, who was and is and*
> *is to come. (Revelation 4:8)*

Hallelujah! For the Lord our God the Almighty reigns.
Let us rejoice and exult and give him the glory, for the marriage of
the Lamb has come, and his bride has made herself ready; to her it
has been granted to be clothed with fine linen, bright and pure—
for the fine linen is the righteous deeds of the saints. (Revelation
19:6–8)

As we kneel before our king as St. John did on the isle of Patmos, we will feel the right hand of Christ on our shoulder. Christ will raise us up, look us in the eye, and finally we will see his face! Christ will say: "Well done, good and faithful servant, because thou hast been faithful over a few things, I will place thee over many things: enter thou into the joy of thy lord" (Matthew 25:21, Douay-Rheims).

Christ is the very height of human aspirations. He is the object of our hopes and prayers. He confers meaning on human events. He gives value to human actions. He is the joy and fullness of every heart. He is the wellspring of our true happiness, the origin of our spiritual and moral life. He tells us what has to be done, and he gives us the strength and grace to do it. For us Christ is everything. To recognize, proclaim, and celebrate Christ is a duty required by faith and the deep need of our human consciousness. Our destiny, our very salvation, is tied to Christ.

Our task today in the New Evangelization is to make the kingdom of Christ present in the lives of persons and in society where they carry out their activities, seeking, as St. Paul says, "that God be all in all" (1 Corinthians 15:28).

For this reason, Christianity is a way of life that is profoundly contemplative and at the same time decidedly apostolic. It is the way in which the faithful live with charity, joy, and authenticity, as well as with a sense of time and eternity. Christianity is the way to live out our status as baptized Christians, fulfilling the duties of our state in life, and being leaven in our own families, in the Church, and in our professional and social milieus.

Christ invites us to journey with him, to take his hand and walk with him as the disciples did at Emmaus. His wish is that all of us can see his face. His last words to us in the Bible are an invitation. They are not a command or a warning, but rather a loving invitation. May all Christians see their vocation in life as a call of love! The Beloved says to us, his bride: "Come!"

> *The Spirit and the bride say, "Come." And let everyone who hears say, "Come." And let everyone who is thirsty come. Let anyone who wishes take the water of life as a gift.*
> *(Revelation 22:16–17)*

Acknowledgments

A heartfelt thank you to all those who walked with me during the writing of this book, especially the following: Jana, Becca, Katelyn, Eleanor, Donna, Lucy, Claudia, Doug, Juliana, and DJ.

Per Regnum Christi Ad Gloriam Dei